Tort Law in Quebec

Tort Law in Quebec

Jean-Louis Baudouin

This book was originally published as a monograph in the International Encyclopaedia of Laws/Tort Law.

Founding Editor: Roger Blanpain
General Editor: Frank Hendrickx
Volume Editor: Britt Weyts

Wolters Kluwer

Published by:
Kluwer Law International B.V.
PO Box 316
2400 AH Alphen aan den Rijn
The Netherlands
E-mail: international-sales@wolterskluwer.com
Website: lrus.wolterskluwer.com

Sold and distributed in North, Central and South America by:
Wolters Kluwer Legal & Regulatory U.S.
7201 McKinney Circle
Frederick, MD 21704
United States of America
Email: customer.service@wolterskluwer.com

Sold and distributed in all other countries by:
Air Business Subscriptions
Rockwood House
Haywards Heath
West Sussex
RH16 3DH
United Kingdom
Email: international-customerservice@wolterskluwer.com

ISBN 978-94-035-0841-2

e-Book: ISBN 978-94-035-0842-9
web-PDF: ISBN 978-94-035-0843-6

This title is available on www.kluwerlawonline.com

The Author

The Honourable Jean-Louis Baudouin obtained his BCL degree from McGill University, Montreal, in 1958, and a PhD from Université de Paris in 1962. He joined the Law Faculty of Montreal University in 1962, where he taught with distinction for twenty-five years until his nomination to the Quebec Court of Appeal in 1989. Having left the Court in 2008, he is presently counsel for the international firm Fasken.

The Honourable Baudouin was a member of the Quebec Bar from 1959 to 1989, Vice-President of the Law Reform Commission of Canada from 1976 to 1980, Queen's Counsel in 1978, counsel to various law firms until 1989, and special consultant on bioethics since 1980. He is Vice-Chairman of l'Institut international de droit d'expression française and former Chairman of l'Association Henri Capitant, section québécoise.

The Honourable Baudouin is the author of '*Produire l'homme: de quel droit?*'; '*Éthique de la mort et droit à la mort*'; and author or co-author of '*Les Obligations*', 1970, 1983, 1989, 1993, 1998, 2002, 2007, and 2014; '*La Responsabilité Civile*', 1973, 1985, 1990, 1994, 1998, 2005, 2007, and 2014; le Code civil annoté du Québec since 1995; le Petit Code civil du Québec since 1994; et le Petit Code civil du Bas-Canada from 1974 to 1993; 'Secret professionnel et Droit au secret', 1965; '*Terrorisme et Justice*', 1970; and co-editor of '*Canadian Bar Review*' from 1980 to 1989.

He is a member of the Royal Society of Canada, Academician of l'Académie des lettres du Québec, Academician of the International Academy of Comparative Law, and Academician of Academia Puertorriquena de Jurisprudencia y Legislacion de Puerto Rico.

He received a doctorate of Law honoris causa of l'Université de Sherbrooke (Canada); l'Université René Descartes, Paris V (France); l'Université Notre-Dame de la Paix, Namur (Belgique); l'Université d'Ottawa (Canada); l'Université Jean Moulin of Lyon (France); McGill University (Canada); and Montpellier University (2014).

In 2001, he received le prix Yves Pélicier, presented by the International Academy of Law and Mental Health, in recognition of his major contributions in medical ethics, legal medicine, and mental health law reform.

The Author

In 2012, he received the highest rank in the Ordre du Québec, was named Officer of the Order of Canada, and in 2015, the rank of Officer of the Order of Canada.

He is now counsel with Fasken.

Table of Contents

Table of Contents

List of Abbreviations

CA	Court of Appeal
Cass.	Cour de Cassation (France)
CCLC	Civil Code of Lower Canada
CcQ	Civil Code of Quebec
Cr. C.	Criminal Code
CSC	Supreme Court of Canada
KB	King's Bench (Court of Appeal)
QCCA	Quebec Court of Appeal Cases
QCCQ	Quebec Court Cases
QCCS	Quebec Superior Court Cases
RSQ	Revised Statutes of Quebec
SCR	Supreme Court Reports

List of Abbreviations

General Introduction

§1. Historical Background

1. Canada is a federal state divided into ten provinces and three territories. Whereas nine provinces and the three territories are of common law tradition, having adopted a regime of civil liability based on tort law and governed by a regime drawn mostly from English sources, the Province of Quebec clearly belongs to the Romanist and civilian tradition derived mostly from French law.

2. The first Civil Code of Quebec (CcQ) (then known as the Civil Code of Lower Canada (CCLC)) came into force in 1866. It was thought, at that time, that codification was the best way of ensuring both the survival of the French legal and cultural heritage and the preservation of the civilian system against potential encroachment of the Anglo-American common law in this part of Canada. Its main source of inspiration was the then-existing French Civil Code of 1804, as well as the French jurisprudence built up for more than fifty years. Yet, the Quebec codifiers did not hesitate to depart from the French solutions where they thought it was necessary to reflect their own national culture and tradition.[1] For instance, the drafting of Article 1053 CCLC was different from that of its counterpart, Articles 1382 and 1383 of the Napoleonic Civil Code. Article 1053 CCLC reads as follows:

'Every person capable of discerning right from wrong is responsible for the damage caused by his fault to another whether by positive act, neglect or want of skill.'

3. The CCLC contained originally only four articles dealing with extracontractual or delictual liability (Articles 1053 through 1056 CCLC). However, five more were added over the years: Article 1054.1, concerning the liability of tutors and curators; Articles 1056a and 1056d, prohibiting civil actions as soon as workers' compensation and automobile accident compensation legislations were adopted; Article 1056b, protecting victims from unconscionable transactions entered into within fifteen days of the accident; and finally Article 1056c, dealing with legal interests payable on the final award of damages.

4. Articles 1053, 1054, and 1055 CCLC dealing, respectively, with the general principles of liability for one's act, with liability for acts of others (children,

1. J. Brierley, *Quebec's Civil Law Codification Viewed and Reviewed*, 14 McGill L.J. 521 (1968) ; and 'Droit québécois et droit français: communauté, autonomie, concordance', Association Henri Capitant (Cowansville: Éditions Yvon Blais, 1993).

employees), with liability for things under one's care, and with liability of animal and building owners were directly drawn from French sources. Again, they were not strictly identical to the corresponding articles of the Napoleonic Code, however, and were sometimes interpreted differently by Quebec courts. In a number of cases (liability for things under one's care, more particularly), Quebec jurisprudence clearly departed from that of France. The Quebec courts, unlike their French counterparts,[2] required for the application of the presumption of fault against the guardian of a thing that the condition caused the damage by its autonomous act, and that, at the time, the thing was not under direct human control.[3]

5. Article 1056 CCLC, whose incorporation in the CCLC is still a mystery, was apparently taken from an English statute.[4] It limited recovery in cases of wrongful death to the married consort, ascendants, and descendants. Under the common law, at that time, death of the victim put an end to any claim against the tortfeasor (*actio personalis moritur cum persona*). The Lord Campbell's Act changed this rule, but in a limited way, by granting a right of action only to the consort, the ascendants, and descendants. At the same period, under French law, anyone who could prove a direct sustainable claim in damage due to the death of the victim was allowed financial compensation. An early Supreme Court of Canada (CSC) case clearly erred in its interpretation of the text[5] and, referring to English common law precedents, refused to extend wrongful death recovery to other persons (such as brothers, sisters, or other relatives), construed this article totally out of context, and also disallowed any form of compensation for *solatium doloris* (i.e., the moral prejudice suffered by surviving family members). One of the reasons given by the Court was to ensure a uniform rule on wrongful death throughout Canada. However, the Supreme Court in a later decision reversed itself and the law now allows compensation for moral damages.[6]

6. Over the years, specific regimes of liability were added by the legislator. First, a distinct workers' compensation scheme, inspired by the German and French models, came into effect in 1909.[7] Workmen and their dependants were, for the first time, compensated for damages resulting from injuries and death without having to prove fault or negligence on the part of the employer. This legislation has been repeatedly amended since, but still holds true to the basic principle that no recourse can be brought before the regular courts on the one hand, and, on the other hand, that compensation is awarded according to a predetermined schedule or tariff.[8]

2. Cour de Cassation (France) (Cass.) Ch. Civ. 21 Feb. 1927, 5-27-1-137 (Arrêt Jand'heur).
3. *Curley v. Latreille*, King's Bench (KB) 31 (1921): 374; Supreme Court Reports (SCR) 60 (1920): 131; *Lacombe v. Power* [1928], SCR 409. *See infra* paras 160 and ff.
4. Lord Campbell's Act, known as the Fatal Accident's Act; 9 and 10 Vict. Ch. 93.
5. *Canadian Pacific Railway v. Robinson* [1890], 14 SCR 105.
6. *Augustus v. Communauté urbaine de Montréal* [1996], 3 SCR 268.
7. *Loi des accidents du travail*, 1909, 9 Edn, VII, Ch. 66.
8. *An Act Respecting Industrial Accidents and Occupational Diseases*, Revised Statutes of Quebec (RSQ), Ch. A-3.001.

7. Second, early in the history of civil liability in Quebec, automobile accident compensation legislation was also adopted.[9] As a matter of fact, it is said that Quebec was the first jurisdiction in the world to do so. The various successive regimes created first a presumption of fault, then of strict liability against the owner and the driver of a motor vehicle, but still left it to the regular courts to determine the extent of liability as well as the compensation award.

8. In 1977, however, despite a strong opposition from both the Bar and the insurance industry, a new system of no-fault came into effect, based on the following principles. First, no claim for personal injuries can be brought before the courts. Second, fault is no longer in issue and compensation is always paid, regardless of the behaviour of the victim. Third, compensation is paid by an administrative body according to certain predetermined and fixed rules and methods of calculation, not unlike those under the workers' compensation scheme. As far as material damages are concerned, recourse can still be had to courts, but a convention entered into by all the insurance companies has had the effect of practically abolishing completely judicial recourses.

9. Third, a number of other specific statutes have introduced identical or similar systems to compensate victims of criminal and good Samaritan acts.[10]

10. On 1 January 1994, a new Civil Code, known as the CcQ, came into effect. This Code has had an international impact, and a number of countries in the world have now adopted some of its provisions, mostly in the area of obligations, special contracts, and civil and commercial securities. Sections 1457 through 1481 CcQ deal with civil liability. By and large, the 1994 Civil Code codifies the basic solutions arrived at by the case law under the old Code and does not depart significantly from the previous tradition.[11] It innovates, however, in two different ways. First, it codifies a number of rules that, under the previous regime, were exclusively jurisprudential, for instance, Articles 1478 through 1481 CcQ dealing with apportionment of liability. Second, it adds new rules to the then-existing law. Article 1471 CcQ (the good Samaritan exception) is an illustration.

§2. Scope of Delictual Liability

I. Contractual and Delictual Liability

11. Unlike French law, Quebec law has experienced serious difficulties in attempting to clearly separate the contractual and the extracontractual or delictual

9. *See infra* paras 186 and ff.
10. *An Act Respecting Assistance for Victims of Crime*, RSQ, Ch. I-6; *An Act to Promote Good Citizenship*, RSQ, Ch. C-20.
11. J. Brierley, *The Revival of Quebec's Distinct Culture: The New Civil Code of Quebec*, 42 U. of T. L.J. 484 (1992).

regimes of liability.[12] Under the CCLC, courts had a strong tendency to treat a number of cases that were really contractual in nature under the delictual or extracontractual regime. This was in the case for medical malpractice cases.[13] Largely ignoring the criticisms of the doctrine, Quebec courts would often be oblivious to the existence of a contractual relationship between physician and patient and resolve the issues of liability and compensation under the delictual regime. Such was also the case, but to a lesser degree, in transportation cases.[14]

12. The CSC had encouraged this approach by deciding in two important cases:[15] despite the existence of a contractual relationship between two persons, the defendant could still be sued in tort if the contractual obligation transgressed was not explicitly set forth in the agreement, but was of an implied nature. In the *Wabasso* case, for instance, the buyer of a machine that caught fire and caused extensive material damages was successfully sued in tort, because the failure to warn the buyer of the potential danger was not clearly mentioned in the contract of sale, but arose from an implicit obligation, related to the general nature of the agreement. These judgments were severely criticized by the doctrine.[16]

13. Under the new CcQ, it is no longer possible to select one regime or the other, where both parties are held by a contractual relationship. A Court of Appeal (CA) case, however, ruled that, because the practice of medicine is now socialized and under government control, the liability is no longer one in contract but that the rules of delictual responsibility do apply to malpractice cases.[17] Nor is it possible any longer for the plaintiff to select among both regimes the specific individual rules that are more favourable to him or her.

14. The contractual and the delictual regimes of liability still present, under the CcQ, some important differences both as to substantive rules (e.g., in contract, only foreseen or foreseeable damages can be claimed) and as to procedure (jurisdiction of the tribunal) with the application of solidarity and limitation periods. The CcQ has, however, considerably reduced the differences that existed between the two. Article 1458 CcQ goes directly against the rule set by the previously mentioned CSC cases and specifically prevents a party to a contract from avoiding the application of the contractual regime and opting for the delictual rules, even if they are more favourable.

---

12. J.-L. Baudouin, P. Deslauriers, and B. Moore, *La responsabilité civile*, 8th edn, *supra*, Nos 1–45 and ff., 29 and ff.
13. *See* the criticism of P.-A. Crépeau, 'Des régimes délictuel et contractuel de la responsabilité civile en droit canadien', *R. du B.* 22 (1962): 501.
14. P.-A. Crépeau, 'Réflexions sur le fondement juridique de la responsabilité du transporteur de personnes', *McGill L.J.* 7 (1960): 225.
15. *Wabasso Ltd v. National Drying Machinery Co.*[1981], 1 SCR 578; and *Air Canada v. McDonnell Douglas Co.*[1989], 1 SCR 1554.
16. *See* as an example: P.-G. Jobin, 'Wabasso: un arrêt tristement célèbre', *McGill L.J.* 27 (1982): 813.
17. *Hôpital de l'Enfant-Jésus v. Camden-Bourgault* [2001], RJQ 832. *See infra* paras 62 and ff.

15. What remains for courts to determine, however, is the type of obligations that can reasonably be qualified as implicit duties resulting from contract and those that can reasonably be said to derive from the general duty imposed by law to compensate for the harm caused by one's fault.[18]

16. The distinction between contractual and delictual responsibilities is largely artificial. The burden of proof, except in those cases where the law specifically provides for a presumption of fault or liability, is identical. Moreover, fault is a concept that applies in a similar way to both contractual and delictual circumstances. The Roman law distinction (which was then thought to be a key difference between the two regimes) between *culpa levis*, *culpa levissima*, and *culpa lata* has repeatedly been rejected by Quebec courts.

II. Criminal and Delictual Liability

17. A number of acts or omissions can qualify both as a civil fault or act of negligence and qualify as a criminal offence (homicide, assault, criminal negligence, theft, etc.). There thus exists a close connection between the civil and the criminal justice systems.

18. The Canadian criminal law system, based on the Canadian Criminal Code, is of British common law origin in terms of substance, evidence, and procedure. The rules devised to establish the guilt of an accused and those necessary to find a defendant civilly liable are thus very different one from another. For instance, criminal law requires guilt to be proven beyond a reasonable doubt, whereas civil liability is established by the mere preponderance of evidence.

19. This fundamental difference between the two systems of justice has given rise to some difficulties. Unlike the French and European traditions, the Quebec case law has been unanimous in keeping the two systems apart and independent one from the other. The French maxim '*le criminel tient le civil en état*' is not a law in Quebec. Thus, a judgment imposing criminal liability is not res judicata for a civil court having to decide whether the same person can also be held to be civilly liable. A criminal verdict is, however, admissible in evidence in a civil trial, and the civil judge is allowed to draw inferences from it.[19] Whereas a verdict of guilty of criminal negligence will most probably preclude a finding by a civil court that the defendant acted in a prudent and diligent way, the reverse is not necessarily true: a person found not guilty of criminal negligence may still be found civilly liable in damages.

18. P. G. Jobin, 'Les ramifications de l'interdiction d'opter. Y-a-t-il un contrat? Où finit-il?' (2009) *88 C.B.R. 335*.
19. J.-L. Baudouin, P. Deslauriers, and B. Moore, *La responsabilité* civile, 8th edn, *supra*, Nos 1–75 and ff., 58 and ff.; *Ali v. Guardian du Canada* [1999], R.R.A. 429 (CA); *La Forcière v. Perras* [1943], SCR 165; and *Sanschagrin v. Lafleur*, 2015 Quebec Superior Court Cases (QCCS) 5101.

20. The Canadian criminal system of justice adopted the plea of guilty, which is in law and in fact, an admission of guilt. Sometimes, however, the accused will enter that plea for personal reasons such as to avoid the emotional stress or economic costs of a trial, while still being innocent. A plea of guilty will create, in favour of the plaintiff, a presumption of fact of the existence of the offence, but not of the liability itself[20] and can be retracted if made by mistake. To sum up, a criminal verdict enjoys a de facto authority before the civil courts having to assess the civil liability of the defendant, but not the full presumption attached to the res judicata.[21]

21. The Quebec system of civil liability can be best divided into two large categories. The first one, the general regime, includes liability resulting from one's own fault, from damages caused by others for whom one can be held accountable, and for damages caused by things under one's care. The rules that apply to these cases are set out in the CcQ. The second one includes an increasing corpus of systems governed by specific statutes that, most of the time, have done away with the notion of fault and adopted a regime of compensation based on the notion of risk or absolute liability (e.g., traffic accidents and workers' compensation schemes).

22. The author, upon the recommendation of the editor, has adopted the uniform outline for the national monographs. It is hoped that this method will be useful and help the comparative process of analysis. However, in a number of cases, there are important differences in qualification and classification of legal norms between the Quebec tradition and the uniform outline. The author has deemed best to regroup under Part III the various cases of damages caused by things, regardless of the type of liability attached to it, for purposes of greater clarity.

---

20. C. Ducharme, 'De la force probante au civil du plaidoyer de culpabilité', *R. du B.* 37 (1977): 512.
21. *See* R. Tremblay, 'L'utilisation successive de la preuve entre les instances civiles, pénales et disciplinaires', CBR 69 (1990): 497; and J.C. Royer and C. Piché, 'La preuve civile' 5th edn., Cowansville, Editions Yvon Blais, 2016, No 803 and ff., 628 and ff.

Part I. Liability for One's Acts

23. There are four basic conditions to the existence of civil liability in Quebec law. First, the defendant must have the mental capacity to distinguish right from wrong (imputability). Second, courts must find the existence of 'a fault'. Third, that fault must have brought about a compensable harm or loss. Fourth, there must be an adequate causal connection between the fault of the defendant and the damage caused to the plaintiff.

24. In Quebec, civil liability can only be imposed on persons who enjoy the mental capacity to foresee the consequences of their acts and omissions and who are able to distinguish right from wrong. This rule is now clearly stated by Article 1457 CcQ. Mental capacity is thus a condition precedent to the existence of civil liability.[22]

25. Traditional Quebec civil law remains true to the principle that liability cannot be imposed without proving the plaintiff's fault. Two exceptions to that rule, however, can be noted. First, the cases under the old Civil Code had identified a number of instances where fault could be presumed (this was the case, *inter alia*, for vicarious liability of employers[23] and for damages caused by a thing under one's care).[24] These findings have now been codified. Defendants face either a presumption of fault (which can be reversed by demonstrating that their conduct was compatible with that of a normally prudent and diligent person placed under the same circumstances) or a presumption of liability that can only be challenged by proof of an act of God or of a fortuitous event. Second, under certain statutory regimes of strict or absolute liability, fault is no longer considered as a necessary element of civil liability.

26. The third basic element of civil liability is the existence of damages suffered by the victim. Even extreme negligence, if it does not cause any harm, will not trigger civil liability, even if it could give rise to criminal liability.

22. *See infra* paras 48 and ff.
23. *See infra* paras 134 and ff.
24. *See infra* paras 154 and ff.

27. Finally, the last element necessary to establish civil liability, under the general regime, is the existence of an adequate causal connection between fault and the damage suffered.[25]

25. *See infra* paras 225 and ff.

Chapter 1. General Principles

28. The system of civil liability in Quebec is based on the concept of fault and not, like in countries that have followed the German tradition, on that of unlawfulness.[26] Such was the case under the regime of the CCLC, and this is certainly still the law under the CcQ of 1994.

29. The notion of fault is a flexible and adaptable concept, fashioned by jurisprudential tradition. The case law of Quebec clearly shows that this concept has proved to have a remarkable capacity to evolve, fluctuate, and adapt itself constantly to the changing social, cultural, and economic context and new legal developments.[27]

30. Fault, not unlike the common law notion of negligence, can be first analysed as the breach of a duty imposed by law. This duty can be found either in a specific statutory provision or in the more general standard of good behaviour prescribed by Article 1457 CcQ, which reads as follows:

> Every person has a duty to abide by the rules of conduct which lie upon him, according to the circumstances, usage or law, so as not to cause injury to another.
> Where he is endowed with reason and fails in this duty, he is responsible for any injury he causes to another person and is liable to reparation for the injury, whether it be bodily, moral or material in nature.
> He is also liable, in certain cases, to reparation for injury caused to another by the act or fault of another person or by the act of things in his custody.

This concept has the advantage of underlining the similarity between contractual and delictual liability, which is apparent from the wording of Article 1458 CcQ:

> Every person has a duty to honour his contractual undertakings.
> Where he fails in this duty, he is liable for any bodily, moral or material injury he causes to the other contracting party and is liable to reparation for the injury; neither he nor the other party may in such a case avoid the rules governing contractual liability by opting for rules that would be more favourable to them.

31. Fault can, however, also be seen as the breach of a minimal norm of behaviour generally acceptable in human relationships. Under that conception, persons are at fault if, by their conduct, they depart from the standard of the model of a normally prudent and reasonable person acting under similar circumstances.

---

26. *See* M. E. Lacroix, *L'illicéité: essai théorique et comparatif en matière de responsabilité civile extra-contractuelle pour le fait personnel* (Cowansville: Éditions Yvon Blais, 2013).
27. *See* J.-L. Baudouin, P. Deslauriers and B. Moore, *La responsabilité civile*, 8th edn. Nos 1–161 and ff., 159. It has been defined in different ways by Quebec authors in Nos 1–162, 162.

32. Thus, the acceptable norm of conduct can either be legislative, in those instances where the legislation itself has set the standard, or jurisprudential, in those cases where courts will identify unacceptable forms of behaviour, incompatible with the conduct that a reasonable person would have held under similar circumstances.

33. At the end of the nineteenth century and the beginning of the twentieth century, an important doctrinal movement in France sought to replace fault as the general norm of civil liability by the notion of risk,[28] which is now, roughly speaking, the equivalent of strict or absolute liability. This attempt had followers in Quebec, who never really succeeded in having it adopted as a general rule. However, the concept of risk is indeed at the very heart of certain specific legislation, for instance that of the workers' compensation scheme and that relating to traffic accidents.[29]

34. Any person who derives an economic or moral profit from the activity of another is, under the theory of risk or strict liability, accountable in damages. Employers are responsible for labour accidents caused to their employees, without the necessity of fault being proven on their part, simply because they derive a financial profit from that economic activity.

35. The theory underlying the compensation scheme for traffic accidents is, however, different. Automobiles represent a serious general risk in society. It is thus socially desirable that compensation of victims, at least for corporeal damages, not be left to the uncertainty of judicial evaluation of the conduct of the would-be tortfeasor. Victims should not be left without compensation for the consequences of this general risk, and the economic burden should be borne by the community as a whole and divided among all the drivers of a motor vehicle.[30]

36. One should add that the modern French doctrine, with the view to protect victims of accidents and to ensure full compensation for their damages, tried to introduce again as a general norm, the concept of *garantie*,[31] according to which the simple interference with corporeal integrity should automatically give rise to compensation. Although, like the theory of risk, it never really took hold in Quebec, it is still, as a general philosophical principle, at the very root of those statutes allowing for compensation of corporeal damages regardless of fault.

37. A concept that recently emerged is known as the precautionary principle. It relates to risk management. While it does not replace fault and is limited to specific areas (environmental law, for instance), it creates potential liability for lack of anticipation of risks that are, however, impossible to determine on a scientific basis, but whose occurrence in the future could cause serious or irreversible damage.[32]

28. L. Josserand, *De la responsabilité des choses inanimées* (Paris: Rousseau, 1897).
29. *See infra* paras 186 and ff.
30. *See infra* paras 186 and ff.
31. B. Starck, *Essai d'une théorie générale de la responsabilité civile considérée en sa double fonction de garantie et de peine privée* (Paris: Rodstein, 1947).
32. *See* J.-L. Baudouin, P. Deslauriers and B. Moore, *La responsabilité civile*, 8th edn. Nos 1–177 and ff., 173; G. Bronner G. and Géhin É., *L'inquiétant principe de précaution* (Paris: P.U.F.), 2010).

§1. FAULT: CLASSIFICATION

I. Contractual–Delictual

38. Articles 1457 and 1458 CcQ codify the rule that contractual and extracontractual fault are but two different illustrations of the same basic notion. On the one hand, parties to a contract are at fault should they fail to perform an explicit or implicit obligation agreed to under the contract. On the other hand, individuals will be liable civilly if they fail to behave, as a normally prudent and diligent person would have under similar circumstances. In the first case, liability relates to the failure to perform a duty voluntarily assumed by the parties, while in the second case, liability results from the failure to act in conformity with an acceptable behavioural standard set either by the legislator or by the courts.

39. As we will see however,[33] a breach of contract giving rise to contractual liability between the parties can also become an extracontractual fault and give rise to delictual liability, where an independent third party suffers damages by reason of the breach.

II. Action–Omission

40. Unlike traditional common law, which is reluctant to impose liability unless there exists a positive duty to act, the Quebec civilian system has always been of the view that fault can result both from an act or omission. The legal duty to act may arise either from a specific legislative provision (such as, for instance, the obligation under the *Quebec Charter of Human Rights and Freedoms* to rescue someone in danger[34]) or from a more general standard, according to which a person is at fault if not acting would be contrary to the standard of conduct that one might expect from a reasonable person under similar circumstances.[35]

III. Intentional–Unintentional

41. In determining whether civil liability exists, the intentional or unintentional character of the act or omission is immaterial. Compensation of the victim for the damage suffered is due, whether it was caused intentionally or not.

42. However, the existence of an intentional fault has some impact on the assessment of damages, more particularly give rise to punitive damages.[36] Also it can be

---

33. *See infra* paras 115 and ff.
34. Charter of Human Rights and Freedoms, RSQ, Ch. C-12, Art. 2; S. Rodgers-Magnet, 'The Right to Emergency Medical Assistance in Quebec', *R. du B.* 40 (1980): 373. N. Kasirer, 'L'expression civile de la solidarité: l'obligation de porter secours en droit canadien et québécois', in *Droits de la personne: solidarité et bonne foi* (Cowansville: Éditions Yvon Blais, 2000), 215.
35. *Nguyen (Succession de)* c. *Site touristique Chute à l'ours de Normandin inc.*, 2012 QCCS 1388.
36. *See infra* paras 257 and ff.

observed from a purely practical point of view that if the fault is proven to be intentional, the plaintiff will not, as a rule, have to prove the causality between the act and the loss suffered; it will be presumed. In certain exceptional cases, for public policy reasons, the Civil Code limits the liability only to intentional acts. This is the case of the tutor, curator, or guardian for damage caused by a person deprived of capacity to act (Article 1461 CcQ) and the case of the good Samaritan (Article 1471 CcQ).

IV. Ordinary–Gross Negligence

43. Unlike Roman law, which adopted different degrees of fault (*culpa levis, culpa levissima, culpa lata*), this notion has never been part of the law of Quebec. However, gross negligence (*faute lourde*), which represents a conduct close to intentional behaviour involving total and wanton disregard for others, is recognized by both the Code and the case law and has a legal impact. On the one hand, while it is permissible and possible, in certain cases, to limit one's liability by contract, such limitation has no effect in cases of gross negligence. On the other hand, while liability insurance will cover damages caused by the ordinary fault of the insured, it will not do so should the fault be intentional or gross.

V. Statutory and Non-statutory Breach

44. When law sets specific standards of behaviour that must be observed in a given situation, any transgression will, in principle, be considered as a fault, giving rise to liability if all the other necessary conditions are met – more particularly, if there is a causal connection between the fault and the damage. The existence of an adequate causality is absolutely necessary. To take a hypothetical example, the mere fact that a person does not possess a driver's licence does not mean that he or she would automatically be held liable for damages resulting from a car accident because there is no necessary causal connection between the absence of the licence and the accident itself. The fault lies in the lack of ability of the driver, not in the possession of a driving license. This is also the case of professional conduct. The fact, for instance, that physicians are charged in discipline does not mean that they would or could automatically be held civilly liable.[37]

45. Conversely, the simple fact that persons have complied with statutory norms does not necessarily mean that they can always escape civil liability because the

37. H. Newman, '*Breach of Statute as a Basis of Responsibility in Civil Law*', 27 CBR 783 (1949); and P.-G. Jobin, 'La violation d'une loi ou d'un règlement entraîne-t-elle la responsabilité civile?', *R. du B.* 44 (1984): 222.

intensity of the duty imposed by courts can, in certain circumstances, be higher than the minimum standard set forth by the legislator.[38]

§2. FAULT: EXPECTED STANDARD

46. To determine whether one is at fault, courts will compare the conduct of the defendant to an abstract model, that is, that of a person reasonably prudent and diligent. The jurisprudential standard of reference is an ordinary citizen and not a person with the highest possible degree of education, intelligence, and ability.

47. Courts will, however, use this abstract model in close relation to the particular factual situation of each case. For instance, to determine whether a physician is liable for malpractice, courts will compare the behaviour of the defendant to that of a normally prudent and diligent physician of the same specialization and take into consideration all particular circumstances: Was it a situation of emergency? Was the illness difficult to detect? Was the prescribed treatment generally regarded as valid by scientific standards?[39]

48. The factual background of each case plays an important role in the evaluation by courts of the conduct of the defendant. For instance, the degree of previsibility that can be expected from individuals may vary considerably.

§3. CAPACITY

49. The problem of the capacity necessary to be held civilly accountable for one's fault concerns three categories of persons: children under age, mentally handicapped, and legal persons.

50. Inability to commit a fault can result from incapacity related to young age or derived from a mental condition that prevents one to be able to distinguish right from wrong or foresee the normal consequences of his or her acts or omissions. The law, however, will not excuse persons who voluntarily or by negligence have brought about their own incapacity, for instance, where they have taken drugs or allowed themselves to be under the influence of alcohol to a point that causes impossibility of realizing the consequences of one's actions.[40] Liability will still be imposed, because this behaviour in itself constitutes a civil fault.

38. *Morin v. Blais* [1977], 1 SCR 570; *Leblanc v. Société de gestion Clifton Inc.* (2002) RRA 525 (SC); *Paquette v. Fédération (La), cie d'assurances du Canada*, 2012 QCCS 4284; and *Ciment du St-Laurent v. Barrette* [2008], 3 SCR 392 (SC).
39. A. Bernardot & R. Kouri, *La responsabilité civile médicale* (Sherbrooke: Éditions Revue de droit, 1980); S. Philips-Nootens, R. Kouri et P. Lesage-Jarjoura, *Éléments de responsabilité civile médicale*, 4th edn (Cowansville: Éditions Yvon Blais, 2016); and R. Kouri & S. Nootens, *L'intégrité de la personne et le consentement aux soins*, 3rd edn (Cowansville: Éditions Yvon Blais, 2012).
40. *Constantineau v. Berger* [1975], SC 211; *Dumulon v. Morin* [1991], RRA 295 (SC); and *B.H. c. Centre hospitalier régional de Baie-Comeau*, 2009 QCCS 585.

51. With young children, the risk of leaving victims without any form of compensation for the prejudice they have suffered is, of course, high and socially undesirable. This is why Articles 1459 and 1460 CcQ[41] impose a vicarious liability on parents and on those who assume a duty of supervision or education of the child (teachers, educators, guardians). A number of precise conditions, however, have to be met. Article 1461 CcQ[42] imposes a similar liability on tutors or guardians of mentally handicapped persons, but only if an intentional fault or gross negligence on their part can be proven.[43]

I. Children

52. Unlike criminal law, which imposes a 12-year-old limit on liability, the setting of a minimum age where a child can be said to be able to commit a fault has been left to the courts to decide. By and large, civil courts ordinarily adopt the age of 7 or 8 as a criterion, but this rule varies with the particular circumstances of each case, and a set breaking point does not exist. Judges will indeed take into account the intelligence and the maturity of the child, as well as his or her degree of education and, to determine liability, will compare his or her behaviour to that of a child of the same age who, under similar circumstances, would have held a reasonably prudent and diligent conduct.[44]

53. If the court decides that the child cannot be held accountable, the victim will then be left without compensation, and the loss suffered will be treated as if it was brought about by a fortuitous event. This, however, does not prevent the plaintiff, as the case may be, from seeking and obtaining compensation from the parents for their own negligence in the education or supervision of the child.[45]

54. A problem arises, however, when the court is of the opinion that the damage was caused both by the combined act of a child who cannot be held liable and by the negligence of a third party. Should the third party then be held for the whole

---

41. Article 1459: 'A person having parental authority is liable to reparation for injury caused to another by the act or fault of the minor under his authority, unless he proves that he himself did not commit any fault with regard to the custody, supervision or education of the minor. A person deprived of parental authority is liable in the same manner, if the act or fault of the minor is related to the education he has given to him.' Article 1460: 'A person who without having parental authority, is entrusted, by delegation or otherwise, with the custody, supervision or education of a minor is liable, in the same manner as the person having parental authority, to reparation for injury caused by the act or fault of the minor. Where he is acting gratuitously or for reward, however, he is not liable unless it is proved that he has committed a fault.' *See* J.-L. Baudouin, P. Deslauriers & B. Moore, *La responsabilité civile*, 8th edn, *supra*, Nos 1–742 and ff., 773 and ff.
42. Article 1461: 'Any person who, as tutor or curator or in any other quality, has custody of a person of full age who is not endowed with reason, is not liable to reparation for injury caused by any act of the person of full age, except where he is himself guilty of a deliberate or gross fault in exercising custody.'
43. *See infra* paras 131 and ff.
44. N. Kasirer, *The Infans as Bon Père de Famille: Objectively Wrongful Conduct in the Civil Law Tradition*, 40 Am. J. Comp. L. 343 (1992).
45. *See infra* paras 121 and ff.

amount of the loss suffered, or only for that part attributable to his or her own fault? Should, on the contrary, the court decide liability and compensation as it would have done had the child been fully capable? After a certain period of uncertainty due to conflicting jurisprudential views, the solution that was finally adopted is the following: the third party can only be held to compensate for the loss of the victim in proportion to the degree of fault he or she has committed and cannot be held liable for the part that would have been assigned to the child, had he or she been held legally accountable.[46]

II. Mentally Handicapped Persons

55. The same rules apply to persons who, by reason of chronic or temporary insanity, are unable to distinguish right from wrong. Incompetence remains a question of fact and is not restricted to the legal notion of incapacity, previously judicially determined by a court when providing the person with a guardian, a tutor, or a curator. Here again, in certain circumstances, the person responsible for the handicapped may be held responsible for lack of supervision.[47]

III. Organizations and Corporations

56. Legal persons or organizations such as corporations, partnerships, trade unions, or associations do not, of course, have a will of their own. They only act through their legal representatives or agents. They can, however, be held liable in the same manner and under the same conditions as a physical person.[48]

57. Their regime of liability is best characterized as a regime of liability for others. They are accountable for damages caused by their representatives, agents, or directors acting for them. Administrators under Articles 371, 2160, and 2164 CcQ do, by their acts, render a corporation civilly liable.

58. It must be pointed out, however, that the legal personality of a corporation cannot be set up as a defence against a person in good faith, where the director or agent has committed a fraud, an abuse of right, or has contravened to a rule of public order. In such cases, the corporate veil can be lifted, and the individual can be held to be personally liable for the damage caused.[49]

46. *Daudelin v. Roy* (1974) C.A. 95.
47. *See infra* paras 131 and ff.
48. Articles 298 and ff., Civil Code of Qubec (CcQ).
49. Article 317, CcQ; *Magasins à rayons Peoples inc. (Syndic de) c. Wise*, 2004 the Supreme Court of Canada (CSC) 68.

59. Trade unions that, in the past century, were denied legal personality for a long period of time can also be sued for their tortious acts and those of their members. Losses caused by illegal strike situations have given rise to a large amount of case law.[50]

50. *See*, for instance, *West Island Teacher's Association v. Nantel* [1988], RJQ 1569 (CA); and *Curateur public v. Syndicat national des employés de l'Hôpital St-Ferdinand* [1996], 3 SCR 211.

Chapter 2. Specific Cases of Liability

§1. Liability of Professionals

I. Medical Practitioners

60. For a long time in Quebec's legal tradition, medical practitioners, hospitals, and clinics were not been frequently sued by patients. This situation has changed considerably since the early 1970s, and there now exists a large corpus of cases on the subject.

61. For a long time also, both doctrine and jurisprudence were divided the nature of the medical liability. While most authors defended the contractual aspect of liability, based on the existence of a consensual relationship between physicians and patients, most of the case law, on the contrary, applied the rules of delictual liability.[51]

62. Medicine, in Canada, was socialized during the early 1970s, and this raised again the issue, albeit in a somewhat different context. Because little was left of the possibility of negotiating an authentic medical contract and because the relevant duties of care on the professionals were now imposed by legislation, could there still exist a real contractual relationship?

63. A CA judgement[52] followed on that score the opinion of a minority of the doctrine[53] and held that the civil liability of physicians should be assessed on an extracontractual basis and no longer on that of a contract. This carries an important practical consequence. Since physicians cannot be held to be simple employees of hospitals, but do act as independent professionals, vicarious liability, for their acts or omissions, cannot be imposed on hospitals, and the presumption of liability for acts of others cannot be involved against them.

64. The standard of care expected from doctors, dentists, and medical personnel in general is that of a prudent and diligent practitioner, placed in similar circumstances. The particular facts of the case play, in this respect, a very important role. Because the obligation is only one of means[54] and not of result, great weight is given by courts to the specific factual context. Did the physician choose the right remedy and use approved and recognized medical practices? Did the patient cooperate with the physician?

---

51. *See supra* para. 11, n. 2. J.-L. Baudouin, P. Deslauriers & B. Moore, *La responsabilité civile*, 8th edn, *supra*, Nos 2–29 and ff., 38 and ff.
52. *Hôpital de l'Enfant-Jésus v. Camden-Bourgault* [2001], RJQ 832.
53. A. Lajoie, P. Molinari & J.-L. Baudouin, 'Le droit aux services de santé: légal ou contractuel?', *R. du B.* 43 (1983): 695.
54. *P.L. v. Benchetrit*, 2010 Quebec Court of Appeal Cases (QCCA) 1505; *J.G. v. Nadeau*, 2013 QCCS 410; *Murgoci v. Laurian* (2004) RRA 432 (SC); and L. Khoury, 'Faute, responsabilité individuelle et medicine modern' in B. Moore Mélanges Jean-Louis Baudouin (Cowansville: Éditions Yvon Blais, 2012: 773).

65. Medical fault can be of four different kinds. The first may occur in the diagnosis process, when the physician gives to the patient a scientific opinion as to what the illness may be. Courts will examine the process and methods used by the doctor to support the diagnosis. The physician will be found at fault if standard medical methods have not been used or a hasty diagnosis without first taking time to have it confirmed by approved scientific tests was given[55] or if the tests have been misinterpreted.[56]

66. Fault can also be found in the treatment administered to the patient. It can occur first in the choice of the treatment. Physicians will be held liable if they choose an inadequate or obsolete form of therapy.[57] Courts will rely on expert evidence for that determination, but have always refused to arbitrate the respective scientific value of different optional treatments, provided they are generally recognized as acceptable by the medical community.[58]

67. Second, physicians can also be held liable for the improper delivery of the therapy. In that respect, courts have repeatedly held that physicians have a continuing duty not only to give adequate treatment but also to monitor it in the follow-up period, so as to foresee and prevent potential negative side effects or the occurrence of risks attached to it.[59]

68. Quebec case law will also hold physicians responsible for breach of professional confidential information. Medical privilege is a fundamental right under the *Quebec Charter of Human Rights and Freedoms*.[60] It covers both the information given by the patient to the physician, within the scope of the professional relationship, and the facts that the physician has been able to observe. However, it was repeatedly held that the right to professional secrecy belongs exclusively to the patient, who may surrender its protection either explicitly or implicitly.[61] The CA has directly confirmed that rule, holding that a physician is under no duty (unless the patient consents to it) to reveal to the direct and indirect family of a female patient the possibility that children born out of her descendants or collaterals could be severely handicapped because of a transmissible genetic disease.[62]

69. Quebec courts also hold medical practitioners liable for the lack of obtaining informed consent from their patients. Consent is a necessary justification to what

55. *Arsenault v. Ryback* [1991], RRA 685 (CA); *Massinon v. Ghys* [1996], RJQ 2258 (SC); *Bouchard v. D'Amours* [2001], RRA 310 (CA); and *Gauthier v. Cordahi*, 2011 QCCS 1115.
56. *Benhaim v. Émond*, 2016 CSC 48.
57. *Cloutier v. Centre hospitalier de l'Université Laval* [1990], RJQ 717 (CA); and *O'Shea v. McGovern* [1994], RRA 672 (CA).
58. *Bérard-Guillette v. Maheux* [1989], RJQ 1758 (CA); *Poirier v. Soucy* [1992], RRA 3 (CA); and *Laurendeau c. Centre hospitalier de LaSalle*, 2015 QCCS 1923.
59. *Cooke v. Suite* [1995], RJQ 2765 (CA); *Drolet v. Parenteau* [1994], RJQ 689 (CA); *Chouinard v. Robins* [2002], RJQ 60; and *C.L. v. St-Arnaud*, 2011 QCCS 2360.
60. *Quebec Charter of Human Rights and Freedoms*, RSQ, Ch. C-12, Art. 9.
61. *Frenette v. La Métropolitaine* [1992], 1 SCR 647.
62. *Watters v. White*, 2012 QCCA 257; and M. Letendre, 'Le devoir du médecin de prévenir les membres de la famille d'un patient atteint d'une maladie génétique', *McGill L.J.* 49 (2004): 555.

would otherwise be a physical and criminal assault. Physicians are thus under the obligation to inform their patients as to the possible and probable risks attached to medical acts and the negative consequences that may arise for the patient. Physicians have been held liable, even though no fault had been committed in diagnosis or treatment, simply for the incidence of their negative, ordinary, and natural consequences, if the patient had not previously been well warned of the possible outcomes.[63] The test applied by Quebec courts in that respect is a subjective one: Would that particular patient, in the specific circumstances of the case, had he or she been properly informed, still have given consent to the medical intervention? The physician must adapt the information given to the specific personal characteristics of each patient. To take an example, a benign surgery, which may yet have negative consequences, on the leg of an ordinary person and on that of a star ballerina carries for them very different consequences and will greatly affect their decisions.

70. Finally, hospitals may also be found liable in damages for negligent acts relating to the safety of patients while they are on the premises.[64] The same holds true for medical services rendered by employees of the hospital (e.g., such as orderlies and nurses).[65]

71. In practice, cases against physicians are very often won or lost on the sufficiency and quality of expert evidence. Over the years, however, courts have increased the importance and use of presumption of facts to alleviate the plaintiff's burden of proof.[66] If, under normal circumstances, the damage would not have occurred, courts will draw a presumption of fact that the damage was not the result of a fortuitous event, but point out rather to the presence of an act of or negligence.[67]

II. Legal Practitioners

72. Quebec, following the French tradition, regulates only two legal professions: lawyers and notaries.[68]

---

63. *Dodds v. Schierz* [1986], RJQ 2623 (CA); *Chouinard v. Landry* [1987], RJQ 1954 (CA); and *Cahill v. Cohen* (2000) RRA 786 (SC).
64. *Rizzo v. Hôpital Notre-Dame* [1975], SC 425; *P.R. c. Centre hospitalier régional de Rimouski* (2005) RRA 37 (SC); and L. de La Sablonnière 'La responsabilité; civile découlant des infections nosocomiales'. Barreau du Québec. Formation permanente, vol. 230 (Cowansville: Éditions Yvon Blais, 2005: 137).
65. *Gravel v. Hôtel-Dieu d'Amos* [1989], RJQ 64 (CA).
66. A. Mecs 'Medical Liability and the Burden of Proof', *McGill L.J.* 16 (1970): 163; P. Nicol, 'Faute médicale: preuve par présomptions de fait et exonération', RDUS 27 (1997): 139; L. Khoury, *Uncertain Causation in Medical Liability* (Cowansville: Éditions Yvon Blais, 2006); and *St Germain v. Benhaim* [2014] QCCA 2207.
67. *Parent v. Lapointe* [1952], SCR 376; and *Benhaim v. Émond*, 2016 CSC 48.
68. J.-L. Baudouin, P. Deslauriers & B. Moore, *La responsabilité civile*, 8th edn, Nos 2–120 and ff., 141 and ff.

A. Lawyers

73. The liability of lawyers is clearly of a contractual nature in regards to their clients. However, they can also be held under extracontractual liability for the damage they may cause to third parties,[69] for instance, defamation either verbal or written for instance in acts of procedure or for engaging in proceedings that are abusive or dilatory.[70]

74. Professional fault can also consist of negligence in professional advice and consultation given to the client. Courts, however, have held that the fault must be a clear-cut one and that no liability will attach for giving an opinion on a controversial matter that is subsequently settled by the courts.[71]

75. Until recently, the number of malpractice cases against lawyers was low. However, it has significantly increased in recent years. The jurisprudence always, however, requires the demonstration of a clear connection between the act of negligence of the lawyer and the damage suffered by his or her client or a third party. Since the final outcome of trials is always uncertain, the client must prove to the satisfaction of the court that had the lawyer acted properly, the chances of winning his or her case were good.[72]

76. The recent Code of Civil Procedure has strengthened sanctions for unnecessary or abusive proceedings and given the courts a large power and a large discretion in that regard.[73] While in most cases the client himself or herself (in his or her capacity as mandator) will be held responsible for abusive proceedings, an increasing number of cases have also applied sanctions to the lawyer personally for unfounded, frivolous proceedings, unnecessary delays, and their use to attempt to defeat the ends of justice (for instance, those known as Strategic Law Suit Against Public Participation).[74]

77. However, a mistake as to the actual state of the law (for instance on a delay of prescription) is, in principle, an act for which lawyers will be held responsible, since they are indeed supposed to have clear and full knowledge of the basic legal rules. If they lack this knowledge, they are expected to take legal advice from specialists.

---

69. *Borenstein v. Eymard* [1992], RRA 491 (CA); and *Daoust v. Bernier* [1992], RJQ 1868 (SC).
70. *Location Panorama Inc. v. Gaucher* [1991], RRA 556 (CA); *Durand v. Martel* [1997], RRA 112 (SC); and *Investissements Pilska Inc. v. Tiramani* [2004], RRA 1186.
71. *Pinard v. Meunier* [1995], RRA 63 (SC). *See also*: *Matte-Thompson v. Salomon*, 2017 QCCA 273.
72. *Doncet v. Doucet c. Fonds d'assurance responsabilité professionnelle du Barreau du Québec*, 2010 QCCS 3005 conf. by 2010 QCCA 2056; and *Lavoie v. Stein*, 2013 QCCS 3471.
73. Articles 51 and ff., CcQ. *See*: R. Lescop. *L'abus de procédure en droit québécois: guide pratique pour l'avocat plaideur* (Cowansville: Éditions Yvon Blais, 2014).
74. *Michalakopoulos c. Sam Levy & Associés inc.*, 2009 QCCA 427; and *2963-0456 Québec inc. c. Performance Guarantees (Québec inc.)*, 2011 QCCS 1460.

B. Notaries

78. Here again the liability of notaries is mainly of a contractual nature. The contract binding notaries to their clients is a mixed one of mandate and services. The notary can act as a legal counsel to one party, in certain circumstances, and as a public officer in others.

79. In his or her capacity of a public officer, the notary, unlike the lawyer, has exclusive legal authority to draft authentic acts that make full proof of their contents (wills, immovable sales, hypothecs, etc.). Should a mistake be made in that respect, the notary can be held liable both in contract to his or her client (e.g., the vendor of an immovable property) and in torts to the other party (e.g., the buyer).[75]

80. The notary's obligations with respect to legal advice and counsel are comparable to those of lawyers. However, notaries do assume an obligation of result with respect to the drafting of authentic acts and the necessary registration procedures that gives effect to them vis-à-vis third parties.

81. To determine whether there is fault, courts will refer to the general norms of notarial practice generally accepted by the profession. However, in one important case, a notary has been held responsible precisely for following a professional practice that the court found to be unreasonable.[76] A large number of cases involve mistakes in the examination of titles of immovable properties.

§2. Liability of Public Authorities

I. Governments

82. The public-common-law tradition in Quebec had historically held, for a long time, that both the federal and the provincial governments were totally free from liability. The maxim 'The King can do no wrong' of English law granted total immunity from civil liability to the Crown and its agents.[77]

83. This tradition has been progressively abandoned, and currently, both the federal and the provincial governments are accountable for the harm or loss they may cause.

84. The liability of the Crown in the right of Canada is governed by a specific federal statute, the *Crown Liability and Proceedings Act*,[78] which has given rise to some difficult legal problems. This statute, instead of setting out the liability of the

75. Y. Marquis, *La responsabilité civile du notaire* (Cowansville: Éditions Yvon Blais, 1999).
76. *Roberge v. Bolduc* [1991], R.C.S. 374.
77. P. Garant, 'Les sources du droit de la responsabilité de la puissance publique', *R. du B.* 66 (1986): 260; and P. Hogg and P. Monahan, *Liability of the Crown*, 4 th edn (Toronto: Carswell, 2011).
78. Crown Liability and Proceedings Act, R.SC (1985) Ch. C-50.

Crown as a general principle, has, on the contrary, listed a series of circumstances under which the federal Crown can be held liable (i.e., for damage caused by a servant of the Crown, by a breach of duty attaching to property, by a motor vehicle, by salvage procedures, and by invasion of privacy),[79] thus remaining true, at least in theory, to the general rule of the Crown's immunity. It also imposes on the claimants specific rules of procedure that are different from those ordinarily followed before the Courts against ordinary citizens, making it somewhat more difficult for plaintiffs, in practice, to seek compensation.

85. The liability of the Crown in the right of Quebec is somewhat different. Under Article 1376 CcQ, the provincial government and its authorities, agents, and representatives, whether they be individuals or Crown corporations, are governed, as any other physical or legal person, by the Civil Code and no longer by the common law tradition and can be held civilly liable as any other person and under the same conditions. Quebec law has thus done away with, both from a theoretical and from a practical point of view, the rule of the Crown's immunity.[80]

86. Article 1464 CcQ reinforces the liability of the provincial Crown by stating that agents or servants of the State or of a Crown's corporation do not cease to act within in the performance of their duties by the mere fact that they perform an illegal or unauthorized act or an act outside their competence.

87. The potential vicarious liability of the State for the acts of public administrators and civil servants has had interesting public law developments. An administrative act may, in certain circumstances, give rise to potential civil liability of the Crown. Courts have held that governments can be held accountable for administrative actions of their civil servants harmful to individuals, and the old rule of total immunity has been severely curtailed by the jurisprudence. A fault in the exercise of administrative powers may also allow for the Crown to become liable for the wrongful exercise of its discretion. Courts, in that respect, however, have followed the English rule set out in *Anns v. London Bourough of Merton*[81] and distinguished between policy and operational decisions.[82] This distinction, as the Supreme Court recently pointed out is, however, not absolute and clear.[83]

88. Municipalities can also be sued as any other person. However, in certain cases, the law provides for the necessity of notices of intention to sue and of shorter prescription periods.[84]

---

79. Crown Liability and Proceedings Act, R.SC (1985) Ch. C-50, Art. 3 and ff.
80. *See* P. Garant, *Droit administratif*, 6th edn (Cowansville: Éditions Yvon Blais, 2013).
81. *Anns v. London Bourough of Merton* [1977], All. E.R. 492.
82. J.D. Archambault, *La responsabilité extracontractuelle de l'État: le politique et l'opérationnel* (Cowansville: Éditions Yvon Blais, 1996).
83. *R. v. Imperial Tobacco Canada Ltée*, 2011 CSC 42.
84. *See infra* para 210.

II. Immunities

89. Several federal and provincial statutes grant, in specific cases, complete or limited immunity from civil liability to a number of persons.

A. Judges

90. Federally as well as provincially appointed judges[85] enjoy full immunity for civil faults for which they could, under normal circumstances, be held liable for, if committed within the regular exercise of their judicial functions. For example, they cannot be held accountable for the consequences of their judicial decisions or for unfavourable comments made to the parties or to a witness during the trial. This total immunity is seen as a necessary condition of judicial independence. Judges may, however, become accountable in discipline before the Canadian Judicial Council or the Quebec Judicial Council as the case may be.

B. Legislators

91. The general rule is that the federal and provincial legislators (the Parliament of Canada and the National Assembly of Quebec) cannot be held in damages for legislative activities that cause damages to a citizen. The opposite solution would be contrary to the principle of the supremacy of Parliament in a democratic society.

92. This rule however is not absolute. The CSC, in the *Manitoba Fisheries* case,[86] held that federal legislation that deprived a private corporation of its commercial activities in favour of a Crown corporation was the equivalent of an expropriation without compensation. In another situation involving the loss of mining rights in a provincial park,[87] the Court also resorted to the theory of disguised expropriation to allow compensation to the aggrieved party.

C. Civil Servants

93. Finally, agents or individuals, acting for the State, may also in certain circumstances be held personally responsible in two cases: first, when they act clearly outside the scope of their functions and second, where their conduct is consonant with bad faith or can be qualified as one of gross negligence. This personal accountability is usually in addition to that of their employer.[88]

---

85. Article 99 of the Canadian Constitution, *An Act Concerning the Privileges of Magistrates*, S.Q. 1982, Ch. 32; and P. Glenn, 'La responsabilité des juges', *McGill L.J.* 28 (1983): 228.
86. *Manitoba Fisheries v. The Queen* [1979], 1 SCR 101.
87. *R. v. Tener* [1985], 1 SCR 533.
88. Y. Ouellette, 'La responsabilité civile personnelle du fonctionnaire', *Admin Pub. Can.* (1976): 1.

§3. Abuse of Rights

94. Article 7 of the Civil Code is to the effect that no right may be exercised with the intent of causing damages to another or in an excessive and unreasonable manner, contrary to the requirements of good faith.

95. The abuse of rights theory has been the object of intense doctrinal and jurisprudential debate in Quebec, too long to examine in detail here.[89] It is not yet really clear whether the doctrine of abuse of rights is only a specific illustration of the notion of fault in the exercise of a subjective right or rather a separate notion, covering cases where the exercise of a right, although done in a perfectly legal way, creates an antisocial effect.

I. Property Rights

96. Insofar as property rights are concerned, courts qualify as abusive conducts those that deliberately seek to deprive one's neighbour of the normal enjoyment of his or her property. This rule has repeatedly been applied by courts, for instance, where a person erected a hideous fence for the sole purpose of depriving his or her neighbour of the view from his or her property.[90] The intent to cause harm is clear, and the right to erect a fence on one's property, although perfectly legitimate, is not exercised in a normal way but only and solely for the purpose of causing harm to another.

97. Courts have gone further and applied the abuse of rights theory to instances where no intentional fault could be found, but where the mere exercise of property rights caused undue and unusual harm to others. This applies to pollution by industries that hold the necessary licences or permits and do their best to diminish the inconveniences caused to their neighbours.[91] The standard used is not the classical standard of fault, but rather that of the antisocial character of the exercise of the property right. This is consonant with the provision of Article 976 CcQ, which states that neighbours have to suffer the normal neighbourhood annoyances that are not beyond the limit of tolerance owed to each other, according to the location and nature of their properties and local customs.

98. In these cases, it is not a valid defence for the defendant to have the necessary administrative authorizations and licences. Nor is the fact that the defendant has occupied his or her property before the plaintiff considered as a bar to injunctive or damages remedies.

---

89. J.-L. Baudouin, P. Deslauriers & B. Moore, *La responsabilité civile*, 8th edn, *supra*, Nos 1–211 and ff., 205 and ff.
90. *Brodeur v. Choinière* [1945], SC 334.
91. *Dugas v. Drysdale* [1894], 26 SCR 20; *Canada Paper Co. v. Brown* [1922], 63 SCR 243; and *Ciment du Saint-Laurent inc. v. Barrette* (2008) 3 RCS 392.

A Supreme Court decision has put an end to the doctrinal and jurisprudential controversy concerning the nature of liability resulting from exercising property rights when no intent to do harm or no negligence can be found. The *Ciment du St-Laurent v. Barrette*[92] case clearly established that the responsibility of the property owner is not based on fault, but is one of a strict and objective nature based on the application of Article 976 CcQ, that is the abnormal character of the prejudice suffered.

II. Procedural and Judicial Rights

99. Quebec courts have long recognized the abuse of rights theory in cases where procedural or judicial rights have been used without discrimination, without reasonable or probable cause, by negligence or malice, and also, of course, in bad faith. There exists in Quebec a large body of cases holding various defendants responsible for malicious, imprudent, or simply negligent seizures of property, denunciations, arrests, etc.[93]

100. The fact that, before acting, the defendant sought legal advice is no excuse and, in certain cases, lawyers may be similarly held personally liable for abusive or dilatory proceedings.[94]

101. The simple fact, however, that a court dismisses an action does not necessarily give rise to recourse in damages for malicious prosecution. Evidence must show conclusively that taking the action in the first place was, in itself, an abuse of process.

Articles 51 and following of the Quebec Code of Civil Procedure gives a vast measure of control to courts on the abusive use of the justice system. Judges can now declare an action, a motion, or a pleading improper, frivolous, dilatory, vexatious, or unreasonable and dismiss it, strike out a number of their allegations, or terminate or refuse to allow an examination of a witness.[95]

III. Contracts

102. Under the CCLC, courts were at first reluctant to apply the theory of abuse of rights in contractual matters. However, by the 1950s, they started to recognize

92. *Ciment St-Laurent v. Barrette* [2008], 3 SCR 392.
93. J.-L. Baudouin, P. Deslauriers & B. Moore, *La responsabilité civile*, 8th edn, *supra*, Nos 1–234 and ff., 221 and ff.
94. *Juneau v. Taillefer* [1992], RJQ 2550 (CA). *See also* the recent amendments to the Code of Civil Procedure, Art. 54.1 and ff.
95. Lescop, R. *Revue analytique de la jurisprudence portant sur les articles 54.1 à 54.6 du Code de procédure civile – Répères – Janvier 2013*; Lescop, R. *Attention, votre poursuite en diffamation vise-t-elle à* bailloner in 'Collection La diffamation' (Cowansville: Édition Yvon Blais, 2013, vol. 16); *L'abus de procédure en droit québecois, Cowansville*, Éditions Yvon Blais, 2014; Acadia *Subaru v. Michaud*, 2009 QCCA 2437; and *Thériault-Martel v. Savoie* [2014] QCCS 3937 (in appeal).

the fact that a subjective right, enjoyed by a contracting party, could, in certain circumstances, be abused and give rise to liability.[96] The Supreme Court in the *Houle v. Banque nationale du Canada* case formally introduced this theory.[97] The CcQ of 1994 has codified a number of jurisprudential solutions and adopted a series of specific new rules concerning good faith, unconscionability of contracts, and abuse of rights in contractual matters, which act as a complement to the theory of abuse of rights.[98]

§4. Injury to Reputation and Privacy

103. Both the Civil Code and the *Quebec Charter of Human Rights and Freedoms* specifically protect a number of fundamental rights and freedoms. Among those, reputation and privacy deserve a specific treatment.[99]

I. Injury to Reputation

104. In the nineteenth and early twentieth centuries, Quebec cases involving defamation and libel relied heavily on a number of common law concepts (such as that of qualified privilege, good faith, and justification or public interest). This is now a thing of the past, and rules assessing liability and compensation for injuries to reputation are dealt with under the general norms and principles of civil law.

105. Any unwarranted attack on the reputation of another, whether it be verbal or written, public or private, may constitute a fault giving rise to an action in damages. The fault can result from an act of bad faith, where the defendant deliberately attacks the reputation of the plaintiff and exposes him or her to hatred, contempt, or ridicule.[100] But it may also occur in cases where the intent to cause prejudice is nonexistent, but the defendant is still guilty of negligence.[101] Moreover, under the civil

---

96. *Quaker Oats Co. of Canada v. Côté* [1949], KB 384.
97. *Banque nationale du Canada v. Houle* [1990], 3 SCR 122. See also *Banque de Montréal v. Bail Ltée* (1992) 2 SCR 554.
98. Articles 1406 and 1435 and ff., Civil Code of Lower Canada. *See* J.-L. Baudouin, 'Justice et équilibre: la nouvelle moralité contractuelle en droit civil québécois', in *Études offertes à Jacques Ghestin: Le contrat au début du XXIe siècle* (Paris: Librairie générale de droit et de jurisprudence, 2001), 29 and ff.
99. Articles 35–41 CcQ, Arts 5–8 of the Charter.
100. R. Morrissette, *La presse et les tribunaux: un mariage de* raison, 2nd edn (Montréal: Wilson et Lafleur, 2004); *Samuelli v. Jouhannet* [1996], RRA 571 (CA); *Hervieux-Payette v. Société St-Jean-Baptiste* [1998], RJQ 131 (SC); *Lafferty, Harwood & Partners v. Parizeau*, [2003] RJQ 2758 (CA); and see 'La diffamation - deuxième colloque' (Cowansville, Éditions Yvon Blais, 2013).
101. *Banque nationale v. Morneau* [1997], RRA 87 (CA); *Beaudoin v. La Presse* [1998], RJQ 204 (SC); *Laforest v. Collins*, 2012 QCCS 3078; and *Gilles E. Néron Communication Marketing Inc. v. Chambre des notaires du Québec* [2004], 3 SCR 95 (SC).

law of Quebec, defamation is not limited to the publication of untrue or false comments, but also of comments relating to situations that are real and true, but that are publicized with the only purpose of causing prejudice to the victim.[102]

106. A great deal of importance is, of course, given by courts to the particular circumstances of each case. For instance, public figures and politicians must show greater tolerance to criticisms as balance must be reached between the protection of the fundamental rights and freedom of expression.[103] The scope of the dissemination of the alleged defamation is also an important factor in the assessment of damages. A number of persons have been granted total or partial immunity. This is the case in the first place for judges and members of Parliament for words spoken in the Parliament or legislative Assembly. Witnesses also enjoy a partial immunity during their testimony in court.

107. Damages for injury to reputation will include not only the economic loss suffered by the defendant, but also moral damages to compensate for the effects of humiliation, contempt, hate, or ridicule the victim has been exposed to. Where the attack is deliberate, both under the Civil Code and the Quebec Charter, supplementary punitive damages can also be awarded.

108. Quebec courts have been less than generous in terms of financial compensation. It is hoped that Ontario defamation cases, which have awarded very substantial amounts of money, will be followed more closely in the future.[104]

109. The Supreme Court in a recent judgement has held that the damage to reputation is of an individual nature and that one person belonging to a group cannot in the name of the others take a class action.[105]

II. Infringement on Privacy

110. The right to privacy includes many different aspects, some of which are listed in Article 36 CcQ: entering or taking anything in one's dwelling; intercepting private communications; appropriating or using one's image or voice in private premises; stalking a person, using one's name, image likeness, or voice for a purpose other than legitimate public information; and using one's correspondence, manuscripts, or personal documents.

---

102. *RBC Dominion valeurs mobilières inc. v. Lizotte*, [1999] RRA 924.
103. *Lafferty, Harwood & Partners v. Parizeau*, [2003] RRA 1145; and *Société St-Jean Baptiste de Montréal v. Hervieux-Payette*, [2002] RRA 727 (CA).
104. *Hill v. Church of Scientology* [1995], 2 SCR 1130; *Botiuk v. Toronto Free Press Publications* [1995], 3 SCR 3; *Cinar v Robinson 213 SCCC 73; and Thériault, Martel, Savoie, 2014 QCCS 3937.*
105. *Bou Malhab v. Diffusion Métromédia CMR inc.*, 2011 CSC 9.

111. The Code[106] as well as specific statutes[107] protects the compilation of records or files on a person. If legitimate (e.g., in cases of credit information), citizens still have the right to examine their record and demand the necessary corrections when the information contained therein is inaccurate, incomplete, or equivocal.

112. Quebec courts have recognized the right to one's image. It is thus forbidden to use the image of another person without his or her consent,[108] unless there is a justification based on the right of the public to be informed.

113. A growing corpus of cases, in the area of the protection of private life, concerns sexual harassment. Sexual harassment exists when two basic conditions are met. First, the conduct must be one that is not accepted by, and is offensive to, the victim. Second, the behaviour of the tortfeasor must have a certain element of repetitiveness.[109]

114. Where sexual harassment in the workplace is the cause of dismissal or resignation of employees, they can claim not only moral damages, but also compensation for the economic loss suffered. Where sexual harassment is caused by the conduct of a co-employee, the employer may also be held responsible on a personal basis (he or she tolerated the sexual harassment) or under the general rule of liability of employers for the acts of their employees (vicarious liability).[110]

115. In recent years a number of class actions have been taken against clergymen and religious institutions for sexual aggressions against children.[111] The legislator in 2013 adopted Article 2026.1 CcQ concerning the prescriptive period for these type of cases. The standard prescriptive period in damages is three years.[112] However, in case of bodily injuries resulting from criminal acts, this period is extended to ten years from the time where the victim became aware that the damage suffered is related to these acts. When sexual aggressions or violent behaviour of a spouse or former spouse is concerned, the prescriptive period is further extended to thirty years.

---

106. Articles 35 and ff. CcQ.
107. *An Act Respecting Access to Documents Held by Public Bodies and the Protection of Personal Information*, RSQ, Ch. A-2.1; *An Act Respecting the Collection of Certain Debts*, RSQ, Ch. R-2.2; *An Act Respecting the Protection of Personal Information in the Private Sector*, RSQ, Ch. P-39.1; and *An Act Respecting Health Services and Social Services*, RSQ, Ch. S-4.2.
108. *Aubry v. Éditions Vice-Versa* [1998], 1 SCR 591; and *Malo v. Laoun* [2003], RJQ 381 (CA).
109. *Commission des droits de la personne du Québec v. Habachi* [1999], RJQ 2522 (CA).
110. L. Langevin & N. Desrosiers, *L'indemnisation des victimes de violence sexuelle et conjugale*, Cowansville, 2nd edn, Éditions Yvon Blais, 2012.
111. *See*, for instance, *Centre de la communauté sourde du Montréal métropolitain v. Institut Raymond-Dewar*, 2012 QCCS 1146; *Tremblay v. Lavoie*, 2014 QCCS 318; and *J.J. v. Province canadienne de la Congrégation de Sainte-Croix*, 2015 QCCS 3583.
112. Article 2925 CcQ.

§5. Interference by Third Persons with Contractual Relationship

116. Contracts are juridical acts between the contracting parties. They are also considered as a juridical fact that third parties cannot simply ignore and must respect.

117. Quebec courts have, in a number of cases, held third parties liable who wrongfully ignored the existence of contractual duties between other parties to their advantage or induced the breach of the contract by one of the parties.[113]

118. This is the case, for instance, where the contract contains a restrictive covenant imposing a duty on one of the parties not to compete with the other for a limited time and a given territory after the expiry of the contract.[114] The third party who wilfully lets the former employee breach that clause becomes liable in tort to the former employer.[115]

119. This is also the case where an individual buys something which he or she knows has already been sold to another.[116]

120. Third parties may also, in certain circumstances, set up the faulty or non-performance of a contract to which they are not a party, but which caused them a direct prejudice. Such is the case of the seller of a product, who can be held liable for damages caused to a third party while the object is being used by the buyer.[117]

113. *Trudel v. Clairol Inc. of Canada* [1975], 2 SCR 236; and *Dostie v. Sabourin* [2000], RJQ 1026 (CA).
114. Article 2089 CcQ.
115. *Beaulieu v. Bizier* [1988], RJQ 108 (CA).
116. Article 1397 CcQ.
117. *See infra* paras 202 and ff.

Part II. Liability for Acts of Others (Vicarious Liability)

121. Responsibility for the negligent acts of others, also known as vicarious liability, is based on two fundamental policy reasons. The first is a social one: by adding another potential debtor with probably stronger financial resources, the law acknowledges the fact that victims should not, generally, be left without any form of compensation.

122. The second is a legal one: all of the persons held to vicarious liability (parents, employers, tutors, guardians, curators) assume towards the authors of the negligent act (children, employees, mentally handicapped persons) a position of control and have a duty of supervision.

Chapter 1. Parents, Educators, and Guardians

§1. Parents

123. Article 1459 CcQ[118] states that those who exercise parental authority over their children are responsible for damages caused by the act or by the fault of their children under age.

124. Divorce or separation does not change the legal tie between the parents and the child, because both continue to hold parental authority, even if custody is given only to one of them. However, the parent who does not have exclusive custody rights will probably not be held liable for damages caused by a lack of supervision, when the child is not under his or her direct control.

125. Vicarious liability of parents extends not only to behaviour that can qualify as a civil fault, but also to the wrongful act of the child, which cannot be qualified as such, but still causes damage. Article 1459 CcQ is the codification of a rule previously set out by case law[119] that extended compensation to victims in cases where, due to young age or lack of mental capacity of the children, they could not be held in law to be accountable and at fault.

126. In theory, children can still be sued personally and remain responsible for the loss.[120] In practice, however, because of their usual lack of financial resources, they are very seldom taken to court.

127. Three main conditions are necessary for the application of this regime. First, the plaintiff must prove the filiation of the child, which, in practice, does not cause any problem. Second, at the time the damage was caused, the child must have been under age, and third the existence of a fault or a wrongful act of the child that caused prejudice to the plaintiff must be proven.

128. Article 1459 CcQ creates against the parents or the tutor a presumption of fault based on the premise that because they hold parental authority, there exists a necessary connection between the wrongful act or the fault of the child and negligence on their part in education or supervision.

129. Parents can exonerate themselves by showing that they gave the child a good education and that their supervision was adequate under the circumstances. In

118. Article 1459: 'A person having parental authority is liable to reparation for injury caused to another by the act or fault of the minor under his authority, unless he proves that he himself did not commit any fault with regard to the custody, supervision or education of the minor. A person deprived of parental authority is liable in the same manner, if the act or fault of the minor is related to the education he has given to him.'

119. *Laverdure v. Bélanger* [1975], SC 612; and J.-L. Baudouin, P. Deslauriers & B. Moore, *La responsabilité civile*, 8th edn, *supra*, Nos 1–742 and ff., 773 and ff.

120. Article 164 CcQ.

assessing liability, courts will take a great number of variable factors into consideration (age, social milieu, temper of the child, type of education given by the parents, undue tolerance for the use of dangerous things by the child, the foreseeability of the child's behaviour, etc.). Each case is really determined on its own merits and according to particular circumstances.[121] They also give great weight to the negligence of parents resulting from too much freedom given to the child, from tolerance of repetitive dangerous behaviour, or from their lack of control over the use of dangerous objects by the child.[122]

130. By and large, Quebec courts tend to exonerate parents for the acts of children who are near the age of majority, unless there is evidence of a clear fault in the education of the child. It is to be noted that a number of legislative provisions give extensive powers to the minor at the age of 14.[123]

§2. EDUCATORS

131. Under Article 1460 CcQ,[124] persons who do not have parental authority over children, but who are nevertheless entrusted with their custody, supervision, or education, are similarly responsible for damages caused by them. One important restriction applies, however, when services are rendered on a gratuitous basis or done for a simple reward (the babysitter is a good example). The educator can only be held responsible for the fault of the child and not simply for his or her wrongful act.

132. It is sometimes difficult to determine with precision which of the parents or of the educators should ultimately be held responsible. For example, damages caused by a child at school can be due either to an inadequate education given by the parents or to a lack of acceptable supervision by the school authorities or to both.

---

121. *See* J. Boucher, 'Minorité et responsabilité: essai de sociologie juridique', RJT 2 (1967): 437; and *Murphy v. Constantineau*, 2015 QCCS 1093.
122. J. Boucher, 'Minorité et responsabilité: essai de sociologie juridique', RJT (1967): 432; and N. Desrosiers, 'La responsabilité de la mère pour le préjudice causé par son enfant', *C. de D.* 36 (1995): 61.
123. Articles 156 and ff CcQ.
124. Article 1460: 'A person who, without having parental authority, is entrusted, by delegation or otherwise, with the custody, supervision or education of a minor is liable, in the same manner as the person having parental authority, to reparation for injury caused by the act or fault of the minor. Where he is acting gratuitously or for reward, however, he is not liable unless it is proved that he has committed a fault.' *See* R. Kouri, 'Réflexions sur la responsabilité civile de la personne non titulaire de l'autorité parentale pour le fait ou la faute des mineurs', in *Mélanges Roger Comtois* (Montréal: Éditions Thémis, 2007), 355.

§3. GUARDIANS: TUTORS AND CURATORS

133. According to Article 1461 CcQ,[125] tutors or curators to a person of full age not endowed with reason are only liable for deliberate or gross negligence in the exercise of their custody.

134. Moreover, under Article 1462 CcQ, a necessary condition to the liability is that the act of the person not endowed with reason would otherwise have been considered wrongful if it had been performed by a mentally apt individual.

135. This is a new addition to Quebec law. The elimination of vicarious liability in circumstances involving only acts of ordinary negligence was thought necessary to encourage voluntary tutorship or guardianship by family members.

125. Article 1461: 'Any person who, as tutor or curator or in any other quality, has custody of a person of full age, who is not endowed with reason, is not liable to reparation for injury caused by any act of the person of full age, except where he is himself guilty of a deliberate or gross fault in exercising custody.'

Chapter 2. Employers (Vicarious Liability)

136. Article 1463 CcQ[126] holds employers accountable for damage caused by their employees, agents, or servants in the performance of their duties.

§1. Origin and Sources of Liability

137. The nature, extent, and limits of the vicarious liability of employers were the object of intense jurisprudential and doctrinal discussions at the end of the nineteenth and beginning of the twentieth century.[127] Courts first required from the plaintiff the demonstration and precise identification of a fault on the part of the employer, for instance, as to the choice or selection of the employee. Subsequently, the cases read into former Article 1054 CCLC a simple presumption of fault: once the fault of the employee had been proved, a presumption of fault could be opposed to the employer. Finally, courts transformed that presumption of fault into one of strict liability, under which employer could only be exonerated by showing that one of the conditions necessary to the existence of the regime had not been met. Employers could no longer exonerate themselves simply by general evidence of adequate supervision of the agent or employee.

138. Article 1463 CcQ codifies the jurisprudential solutions arrived at under the old Civil Code and endorses the absolute vicarious liability theory. Proof, by the plaintiff, of a fault on the part of the employer is no longer a condition precedent to the application of the presumption of liability. It is, of course, still necessary for the victim to prove the existence of a fault of the employee.

139. The policy basis for the imposition of a regime of strict liability is clearly of a social nature. Since employers generally derive economic benefits from the activities of their employees, the necessary social counterpart is to hold them responsible for the harm that they may cause and thus ensure a better chance of compensation for victims; because clearly, the possibility of recovery is higher if employers (who are probably more solvent) can also be sued.

140. From a legal analysis point of view, the basis for liability of employers is really no longer that of fault, as in the general regime, but rather of assumed risk. By using the services of someone to perform what employers could have done themselves, they create a higher potentiality of risks to others and must assume the consequences of his or her realization.

126. Article 1463: 'The principal is liable to reparation for injury caused by the fault of his agents and servants in the performance of their duties; nevertheless, he retains his recourses against them.'
127. J.-L. Baudouin, P. Deslauriers & B. Moore, *La responsabilité civile*, 8th edn, *supra*, Nos 1–813 and ff., 809 and ff.

§2. CONDITIONS

I. Fault of Employee

141. Three conditions must be met to engage the vicarious liability of employers. First, the employee must be at fault. The onus of proof of this first element lies on the plaintiff.

II. Employment Relationship

142. Second, there must exist between the employer and the employee a clear subordination relationship. This second condition has raised some difficult problems. Generally speaking, compliance with this condition requires proof that the agent, servant, or employee acted for the benefit of the employer in a context of dependence of the first on the second.

143. Courts have identified, as a necessary characteristic of that relationship, the existence of a power of control by the employer over the employee, resulting from the right to give orders, to supervise the work, and to indicate how and in what manner a given task should be performed. This power of control must be direct and specific.[128]

144. In that respect, courts have repeatedly held that professionals, in particular, health professionals (physicians and surgeons), working out of a hospital cannot be held to be agents or employees of the institution, because hospitals have authority neither to dictate to them how to treat a patient, nor to give them orders in that respect.[129]

145. The precise identification of this power of control is largely a question of fact, and solutions do vary according to the particular circumstances of each case.

146. One method of identification is to examine the contractual relationship between the two parties. Contracts of employment, of lease and hire of services,[130] and of mandate,[131] generally give a specific power over the employee and agent.

147. However, and by contrast, a contract of services does not.[132] A general contractor, for example, cannot be held to be the employee of the client for whom a

128. *Quebec Asbestos Co. v. Couture* [1929], SCR 166.
129. J.P. Ménard & D. Martin, *La responsabilité médicale pour la faute d'autrui* (Cowansville: Éditions Yvon Blais, 1992); and D. Chalifoux, 'Vers une nouvelle relation commettant-préposé', *R. du B.* 44 (1984): 815.
130. Article 2098 CcQ and ff.
131. Article 2130 CcQ and ff.
132. *Kerr v. Atlantic and North West Railway Co.*[1895], 25 SCR 197; and *Quebec Asbestos Co. v. Couture* [1929], SCR 166.

building will be erected, because even if the client has a general say in the execution of the work, the entrepreneur remains the own master for the performance of the contract. This independence is incompatible with the degree of power of control required to justify the existence of vicarious liability.

148. The subordination relationship is not, however, exclusively dependent upon the existence of a contract. Courts have held that persons who, even fortuitously, agree to perform a task for another, under supervision and orders (e.g., members of the family), in the absence of an express or implied contractual relationship, can still qualify as agents or employees and justify the imposition of vicarious liability.[133]

149. In certain instances, the services of a permanent employee will be temporarily lent to another for the performance of a specific task. In such cases, the person liable will be the one who, at the time the damage was caused, had the real and effective power to give orders to the employee and could exercise direct supervision over the performance of the work.[134]

III. Performance of Duties

150. The third condition is that the damage must have been caused during the performance of the duties of the employee. This condition has also given rise to difficulties.

151. First, generally speaking, courts will not consider that a criminal act committed by the employee within the general framework of the employment is sufficient, in itself, to exonerate the employer, under the pretext that it could not have been foreseen or tacitly authorized by the latter. For instance, the fact that an employee assaults a client of the employer does not exonerate the later if the act was still committed within the general framework of the performance (of course, deviant in that case) of the employee's duties.[135]

152. The problem is more complex where the employee disobeys a specific order given by the employer. The case law, here again, holds that the mere disobedience to an express order can only discharge the employer from liability if, in so doing, the employee has clearly stepped outside the scope of the performance of his

133. *Majeau v. Majeau* [1986], RRA 69 (CA); and *Travellers of Canada v. Legault* [1994], RRA 236 (CA).

134. *Hôpital Notre-Dame v. Villeneuve* [1970], CA 538; and *L. S. v. Centre hospitalier affilié universitaire de Québec – Hôpital de l'Enfant-Jésus*, 2009 QCCS 1622.

135. *Hudson's Bay Co. v. Vaillancourt* [1923], SCR 414; *Franck de Rice v. Elder* [1939], 67 KB 563; *Havre des femmes v. Dubé* [1998], RJQ 346 (CA); *Axa Assurances inc. v. Groupe de sécurité Garda inc.*, 2008 QCCS 6087; and *Québec (Procureure générale) v. Bélanger*, 2012 QCCS 845. *See* L. Langevin, 'Acte criminel de l'employé et responsabilité objective de l'employeur: pour une redéfinition du critére de rattachement', RJT 47 (2013): 31. *See* L. Langevin 'Acte criminel et responsabilité objective de l'employeur: pour une redéfinition du critère de rattachement', RJT 47 (2013) 31.

or her duties. Disobedience or simple transgression as to the way the task has to be performed, does not, per se, set the employee outside the scope of his or her functions.[136]

153. The fact that the damage was caused at the workplace and within the time frame of the employment, however, creates a rebuttable presumption that it was caused within the performance of the employee's duties. The reverse is not true however, because an employee can obviously still be acting for the employer outside the place and time generally set for the performance of the work.

154. To sum up, damages resulting from a negligent performance of employees' duties due to their negligence or incompetence render the employer fully vicariously liable. The liability also extends to cases where the employee purposely or inadvertently disobeys the general structure previously set by the employer, by changing the methods of performance of their work, but still acts for the general benefit of the later.

155. Finally, the only case where employers will escape vicarious liability is where the damage is caused by employees totally outside the general scope of their functions. In such cases, the employee cannot be said to have acted for the general or specific benefit of the employer; and conversely, the latter cannot be held to assume liability. To take an example, this is the case of the bus driver, who, after work, assaults a former passenger who, during a previous trip, had caused some disturbance.[137]

---

136. *Zambon v. Schrijvershof* [1961], SCR 291; *Hreha v. Gordon Vacuum Cleaners Inc.* [1964], SC 316; *Biondi v. Syndicat des cols bleus regroupés de Montréal (SCFP-301)*, 2010 QCCS 4073; and *Montréal (Ville de) v. Biondi*, 2013 QCCA 404.
137. *Co. de transport provincial v. Fortin* [1956], SCR 258.

Part III. Forms of Strict Liability

Chapter 1. General Liability for Things under One's Care

156. The regime of liability for damage caused by things under one's care was of considerable importance in the late nineteenth century, because it was the very basis of compensation for labour accidents before the first Workman Compensation Act came into force in 1909. Moreover, for a certain period of time, it was also used to determine liability for automobile accidents, before this area of civil liability came under specific statutory provisions.[138]

157. Under the regime of the CCLC, a series of Supreme Court decisions gave to the relevant paragraph of Article 1054 a distinctive interpretation and, after a long jurisprudential evolution, finally decided that the victim of a damage caused by a thing enjoyed a presumption of fault against the guardian, that is the one who, at that time, had control over it.[139]

158. In other words, if the damage is caused by the autonomous act of the thing, its guardian is presumed at fault and can only escape liability by proving an absence of fault, in other words, that he or she acted as a prudent and diligent person under the particular circumstances of the case.

159. The Civil Code of 1994 simply endorsed this solution and codified it under Article 1465 CcQ.[140]

§1. Conditions of Liability

I. Damage Caused by a Thing

160. The word 'thing' is not defined by the Civil Code. It has been the task of the courts to give it a legal content. By and large, courts have held that the regime applies both to corporeal objects, such as movable property, and to incorporeal

---

138. *See infra* paras 186 and ff.
139. J-L. Baudouin, P. Deslauriers & B. Moore, *La responsabilité civile*, 8th edn, *supra*, Nos 1–928 and ff., 867 P.-A. Crépeau, 'Liability for Damage Caused by Things from the Civil Law Point of View', 40 CBR (1962): 222.
140. Article 1465: 'A person entrusted with the custody of a thing is liable to reparation for injury resulting from the autonomous act of the thing, unless he proves that he is not at fault.'

things such as electricity, steam, chemical emanations, gas, and water. The practical difficulty in these latter cases is to identify precisely who is the guardian. For example, where harm is caused by electricity, who among the utility company that produces it, the person who uses it or the company entrusted with its transport, can qualify as the guardian?

161. Liability has also been applied to immovables such as lifts, ducts, and reservoirs, but not to buildings *stricto sensu* because they are covered by a particular regime (Article 1467 CcQ).[141]

II. Damage Caused by an Active and Autonomous Act

162. In this respect, Quebec civil law clearly departed from the French interpretation of an analogous article of the Code Napoleon, as interpreted by the famous *Jand'heur* case.[142] This 1927 judgment of the French *Cour de Cassation* decided that liability for things under one's care (and thus the presumption of fault derived from it) could apply where the thing that caused the damage was, at that time, directly operated by human hand. This interpretation allowed French courts to apply the presumption of fault against drivers in traffic accident cases.

163. On the contrary, Quebec case law repeatedly held that the regime of liability for things under one's care applies only to situations where two basic conditions are met. First, the damage must be caused by the autonomous act of the thing, that is the thing must have caused the damage by itself and not by a mere extension of normal human activity. For example, if one shoots another with a gun, this condition cannot be met, because the damage is caused by the extension of human activity. If, on the contrary, a loaded gun laid to rest on a chair falls and injures somebody, the regime will apply and the victim will benefit from the presumption of fault against the guardian.

164. Second, the thing must play an active role in the creation of the damage and not be purely passive. If someone slips and falls on the ice, the ice is, of course, the material cause of the damage, but the ice remained purely passive. If, on the contrary, a piece of ice falls from a roof and injures a passer-by, then the second condition is satisfied.

165. It is not always easy, however, to clearly separate the regime of liability for things under one's care that carries a presumption of fault from the general one that does not. For instance, if a golfer hits a ball that bounces off a tree and injures another, could it really be argued that the damage is caused by the autonomous act of the thing?

141. *See infra* paras 178 and ff.
142. Cass. Ch. Civ., 21 Feb. 1927, S-1-137.

166. A number of authors have criticized the specificity of the Quebec civil law solution in this respect and recommended that it should follow the French experience and rule.[143]

III. Damage Caused by a Thing under One's Care

167. The exact notion of the 'care' of a thing has also given rise to controversies. Care, in general, is consonant with an individual power of control, direction, or supervision over the object itself. Care can be defined as the relationship between this object and a person, based on the power of control that the latter can exercise on it, since whoever controls the thing also has the power of preventing any damage caused by it.

168. Care and ownership often coincide, because owners have, indeed, a direct legal power of control over their possession. Yet, what the law requires is not simply an abstract power, but a concrete factual and realistic one. This, for instance, explains why, if the damage is caused by a thing that has been stolen, the thief and not the owner will be held responsible. The owner, while retaining in law an abstract power, has lost in that case the immediate control over the object and thus the possibility of taking the necessary measures to make sure that no harm is done to third parties.[144]

169. This power of control must also be exercised for the benefit of the person holding the thing. This explains why, if the damage is caused by an object under the physical control of an employee, the employer will still be liable to the victim. The control of the employee is exercised not for his or her own benefit but for that of his or her employer.

§2. Limits of Liability

170. Under the former CCLC, courts had, after a lengthy evolution, finally decided that the general regime of liability for things under one's care created a simple presumption of fault and not one of absolute liability.[145] The 1994 Civil Code endorsed this solution. The plaintiff must thus prove that the damage was caused by the autonomous and dynamic action of the thing and that, at that time, it was under the care and control of the defendant.

171. Once this onus is discharged, a presumption of fault is created that, in turn, shifts the burden of proof.

---

143. M. Millner, *Autonomous Acts of Things in Quebec Law: Legal Adventurism versus Legal Conservatism*, 17 McGill L.J., 699 (1971).

144. *See* K. Antaki 'Garde de structure et garde de comportement, un aspect de la responsabilité du dommage causé par les choses' McGill LJ (1966) 41.

145. *Watt and Scott Ltd v. City of Montreal* [1920], 60 SCR 523; and *Les Fumoirs Mouski inc. v. MRC de La Mitis*, 2017 QCCA 205.

172. The defendant can escape liability however by proving that the damage was caused by an act of God, the fault of a third party for whom he or she cannot be held responsible, or the fault of the plaintiff. In practice, the presumption of fault will require the defendant to identify conclusively the exact cause of the damage. The standard of care required is that which would have been observed by a normally diligent and prudent person under identical circumstances. Knowledge by the guardian of the dangerous nature of the thing, of the existence of defects, and or the abnormal operation of the object are important factors taken into consideration by the courts.

Chapter 2. Liability for Damage Caused by Animals

173. Animals, under the Civil Code, used to qualify as things.[146] However, the Quebec legislature recently adopted an *Act to improve the legal situations of animals.*[147] The law imposes on owners, breeders, and the public in general a duty to make sure that animals enjoy proper care and prohibits a series of acts in connection with their breeding, transport, and training. Under the law, they are given a special status. They can no longer be identified as a 'thing' or personal property, but are considered as living and salient creatures. Here again, the Code, true to the tradition followed by the CCLC, retains a specific provision dealing with the liability for damages caused by them, under Article 1466 CcQ.[148] The legal basis of the liability is the care, custody, and control of the animal. The theory behind it rests on the notion of risk. Owners or possessors of animals create a risk for others and must compensate their victims should it occur.

174. Both the owner and the guardian of the animal are subject to liability. The owner is liable also in damages where the animal has escaped or strayed.

175. The liability, unlike that of the general regime of liability for things under one's care, applies both to the legal owner, caretaker, or custodian of the animal and to the person who, in fact, exercised control at the time the damage was caused and made use of the animal, even if it was for a limited period of time.[149] This would be the case, for instance, of damages caused by a dog under the control of a veterinarian.

§1. Conditions of Liability

176. The liability applies mostly, if not exclusively of course, to domestic animals (e.g., cats, dogs, and horses), but in certain cases, defendants have also been held liable for damages caused by wild animals, where it was shown that they did, in fact, exercise a certain measure of control over them.[150]

177. The damage must have been caused by the conduct or act of the animal, but direct physical contact is not strictly necessary. For example, the owner of an animal that simply frightens the victim and causes a nervous shock could still be held liable.

146. Article 910 CcQ; and J.-L. Baudouin, P. Deslauriers & B. Moore, *La responsabilité civile*, 8th edn, *supra*, Nos 1–992 and ff., 909 and ff.
147. *An Act to Improve the Legal Situation of Animals* (LQ 2015 Ch. 35) amending the Art. 89 of the Civil Code, Arts 898.1, 905, 910, 934, 989, and 1161 and providing for the *Animal Welfare and Safety Act.*
148. Article 1466: 'The owner of an animal is liable to reparation for injury it has caused, whether the animal was under his custody or that of a third person, or had strayed or escaped. A person making use of the animal is, together with the owner, also liable during that time.'
149. *Rivest v. Doré*, 2013 QCCS 153.
150. *Sylvestre v. Lapierre* [1979], CA 268.

§2. LIMITS OF LIABILITY

178. The liability for damages caused by an animal is a strict and absolute liability.[151] In other words, Article 1466 CcQ does not create a mere presumption of fault but an irrefutable presumption of liability. Owners or persons who make use of the animal can no longer exonerate themselves by simply proving that they have generally exercised good control over the animal and that they have acted as an ordinary diligent and prudent person would have under the circumstances.

179. The only possible means of exoneration for them is to prove fortuitous event, the fault of the victim, or that of a third person for whom they cannot, in law, be held responsible.[152]

180. One question that remains unsolved as of now is whether the liability regime of 1466 CcQ would also apply to viruses and bacteria.

151. *Morrow v. Lefrançois* [2003], RRA 39 (CA); and *Dion v. Charette*, 2016 QCCS 5811.
152. *Tokar v. Poliquin*, 2013 QCCS 1889; and *Rivest v. Doré*, 2013 QCCS 153.

Chapter 3. Liability for Damage Caused by Buildings

181. The liability of owners for damage caused by their buildings is found in Article 1467 CcQ.[153]

§1. Conditions of Liability

I. Ownership

182. Unlike the general regime of liability for things under one's care, the liability imposed by Article 1467 CcQ rests only on the owner of the building and not on the person who, at one time or another, may have had the actual control of it (e.g., a lessee). This does not exclude, however, the additional liability of the user, who is not the owner, but under the general regime of liability for things under one's care.

II. Notion of Building

183. The word 'building' has been given a large and extensive interpretation by the courts. Liability has been held to apply to damage caused both by the building itself and by parts of it such as staircases, balconies, walls, roofs, and sprinklers.

III. Lack of Repair or Defect of Construction

184. The liability of the owner is strictly limited to damages resulting either from a lack of repair or from a defect of construction. The collapse of the building, even in part, is the necessary conditions of liability, but only if it results from a lack of repair or a defect of construction. Plaintiff has the onus of proof to identify conclusively the origin of the damage. Courts have held that the owner cannot be held liable if the loss caused by the collapse of part of an immovable is due to the fact that the victim has used it in a way contrary to its initial purpose and destination. This is the case of a window cleaner who uses window sockets that were not designed for that purpose to support his or her equipment or of the person who leans on a window screen and falls.[154] The duty of the owner is limited to build according to the generally accepted norms of construction and to keep the immovable in an adequate state of repair and maintenance.

---

153. Article 1467: 'The owner of an immovable, without prejudice to his liability as custodian, is liable to reparation for injury caused by its ruin, even partial, where this has resulted from lack of repair or from a defect of construction.' *See* J.-L. Baudouin, P. Deslauriers & B. Moore, La responsabilité civile, 8th edn, *supra*, Nos 1–992 and ff., 909 and ff.

154. *Rubis v. Gray Rock Inn Ltd* [1982], 1 SCR 451.

§2. Limits of Liability

185. Article 1467 CcQ, unlike the general regime of liability for things under one's care, does not create a presumption of fault or of liability. The burden of proof thus rests entirely on the victim to prove each and every single condition giving rise to it.[155]

186. Once this is done, however, owners can exonerate themselves only in a limited number of cases. They cannot do so by simply proving that, generally speaking, they acted as reasonable, diligent, and careful persons, or that they were in good faith, or that they had no actual knowledge of the existence of the defect of construction or of the lack of repair of the building.

187. In practice, the only type of exoneration open to them is that the actual cause of the damage was an act of God, the fault of a third person for whom they cannot be held liable, or that of the plaintiff. If held liable, the owner may seek reimbursement by an action in warranty against the builder, the architect, or the person entrusted with the maintenance of the building. He or she may also, vis-à-vis persons with whom he or she entertains a contractual relationship (e.g., a lessee), limit or exclude his or her liability, subject, however, to the general prohibition to do so for personal injuries and cases of gross negligence (Article 1474 CcQ).[156]

155. *Zuchoski v. Intact, compagnie d'assurances*, 2012 QCCS 2686.
156. *See infra* paras 219 and ff.

Chapter 4. Liability for Damage Caused by Automobiles

§1. Historical Evolution

188. The first legislation governing traffic accident cases goes back to 1904. Its purpose was mainly to protect horse-drawn vehicles against the perils of the newly invented automobiles.[157]

189. As early as 1912, however, the Quebec legislature introduced a series of rules on liability, and created a presumption of fault against both the owner and driver of a motor vehicle.[158] This text was amended several times over the years, but did not succeed in solving all the legal and social problems resulting from traffic accidents. For example, it failed to impose mandatory liability insurance, thus leaving a number of victims without compensation.

190. After a major overhaul of the legislation in 1960, which imposed stricter obligations in relation to insurance and created a special fund for the compensation of victims who could not otherwise collect from the responsible party (e.g., in hit and run cases), Quebec finally adopted an entirely new approach in 1977.[159]

§2. General Principles

191. The current legislation concerning traffic accidents is based on four basic principles.

192. The first one is a clear separation between procedures for the compensation of personal injuries and death on the one hand and for property damages on the other.

193. The second is the complete abolition of fault as the basis of compensation for bodily injuries and death and the creation of an absolute no-fault system. Victims of traffic accidents and their dependants in case of death, regardless of their own fault, always have the right to recover damages for personal injuries directly from an administrative body: the *Société de l'assurance automobile* according to a process resembling that of workmen compensation. The tariffs of compensation are set out in various regulations. For property damage (e.g., damage to cars), fault still remains the basis of the liability, at least in theory. In practice, however, insurers

157. *Loi concernant les automobiles*, 4 Ed. VII, Ch. 30.
158. *An Act Amending the Revised Statutes of 1909 Concerning Motor Vehicles*, 3 Geo V, Ch. 19, Art. 2.
159. *Automobile Insurance Act*, RSQ, Ch. A-25; L. Perret, 'La nouvelle loi sur l'assurance automobile du Québec', RGD 9 (1978): 7; and J.-L. Baudouin, 'La nouvelle législation québécoise sur les accidents de la circulation', RIDC 31 (1979): 381.

have agreed among themselves to a direct compensation covenant scheme that predetermines which one shall be liable to pay in all the possible hypothetical cases of traffic accidents.

194. The third basic principle is the complete prohibition to claim damages for personal injuries or death before the courts. The victim of a traffic accident has no choice but to claim from the *Société de l'assurance automobile*, and cannot sue the author of the damage before regular courts, even if only to claim the difference between the actual loss suffered and the amount received from the administrative body.

195. The fourth principle is that every driver must hold a basic amount of insurance covering property damage that may be caused by his or her automobile anywhere in Canada and in the United States.

§3. COMPENSATION SCHEME

196. Everyone – whether they be the driver, a passenger, a pedestrian, etc. – injured in an automobile accident is entitled to compensation. This applies to Quebec residents both for accidents occurring in Quebec and for those occurring elsewhere in the world. Non-residents, victims of an accident in Quebec can also claim from the *Société de l'assurance automobile* in two situations: (1) if they come from a country or state that has signed a reciprocity agreement with Quebec and (2) if the claimant is not at fault.

197. Courts have been very liberal in the interpretation of what constitutes an accident giving rise to compensation. It is not necessary, for instance, that the automobile be involved in what would ordinarily be considered as a collision. It was held, for example, that death due to monoxide poisoning was covered under the law.[160] The death of a person sitting in a parked car caused by the fall of a tree was also held to fall within the scope of the Act.[161] Recently, the Supreme Court in two interesting judgements[162] held that the no-fault compensation scheme applied in the first case where the victim of a traffic accident suffered additional and aggravated damages due to subsequent medical malpractice. In the second case, the victim, because of the fault of the police, had been left without help following a car accident and suffered extensive damages. In both cases the Court refused to apply the traditional approach of causation and the rule of *novus actus interveniens*. Three types of accidents are, however, excluded. The first is that caused while the car is not in motion by a device that can be operated independently (e.g., a winch and a

160. *Co. d'assurance Victoria du Canada v. Neveu* [1989], RRA 226 (CA); and J.-L. Baudouin, P. Deslauriers and B. Moore, *La responsabilité civile*, 8th edn, *supra*, Nos 1–1169 and ff, 1043 and ff.
161. *Ville de Westmount v. Rossy*, 2012 CSC 30; *see also Productions Pram v. Lemay* [1992], RJQ 1738.
162. *Godbout v. Pagé* and *Gargantiel v. Québec*, 2017 CSC 18.

crane). The second are accidents caused by certain types of vehicles (e.g., snowmobiles, caterpillars, and farm equipment vehicles).[163] The third concerns accidents occurring as a result of an automobile contest, show, or race. In these three cases, liability is determined by the ordinary rules of delictual responsibility.

I. Bodily Injuries and Death

198. Victims of personal injuries resulting from traffic accidents can recover from the *Société d'assurance automobile* compensation for economic loss. The indemnity for income replacement will vary in relation to the fact that, at the time of the accident, the victim held a regular employment or not, was self-employed, held a part-time employment, was unemployed but able to work, was under age and in full-time attendance in an educational institution, or, finally, was unable to hold any employment.

199. Victims can also claim up to a maximum figure determined by law for pain and suffering, loss of enjoyment of life, as well as for all the medical and rehabilitation expenses. In the case of death, dependants (broadly defined by law) can claim up to a maximum amount for loss of support and funeral expenses.

200. Indemnities for income replacement are paid every fourteen days in the form of an annuity. Other indemnities are paid by a lump sum award. The procedure before the *Société d'assurance automobile* is very flexible and avoids undue delays in payments to the victims. The administrative process works well in practice, and claimants can even benefit, in certain circumstances, from advanced payment before their claim is processed.

II. Material Damages

201. Insofar as damages to vehicles are concerned, all the insurance companies operating in Quebec have signed a direct compensation agreement among themselves, which predetermines which insurer will be responsible for which accident in each and every possible type of circumstances. Consequently, the owner of the car involved will always claim directly from his or her own insurer, regardless of who is really responsible. The latter will, in turn, if the convention holds that he or she should not be held responsible, claim reimbursement from the insurer of the other party for the money paid to his or her own insured.

202. The compensation scheme adopted in 1977 has, by and large, worked well. Courts are no longer saddled with thousands of cases, and victims can expect to receive compensation within a very reasonable time frame. Moreover, the system is

163. *Club de ski de fond Parc du Mont-Orford v. Egervary*, 2012 Quebec Court Cases (QCCQ) 1865.

efficient, despite the fact that the predetermined indemnities payable are far lower than the amounts that, under ordinary circumstances, could be claimed before the regular courts.[164]

203. Recently, a number of persons have lobbied for an amendment to the existing legislation, authorizing victims of drunk drivers to sue them personally before regular courts and claim their actual damages instead of the lump sums handed out by the *Société d'assurance automobile*. This has met up to now with the resistance from those who believe that it could be the first of a series of exceptions to a social system of compensation that has worked relatively well.

164. T. Rousseau-Houle, 'Les vingt ans de l'assurance automobile sans égard à la responsabilité', in *Actes du Colloque sur l'assurance automobile* (1998). D. Gardner 'Comparer l'incomparable: les indemnités pour préjudice corporel en droit commun et dans la Loi sur l'assurance automobile', CdD 39 (1998) 429.

Chapter 5. Liability for Manufactured Products

204. We are concerned here only with the delictual liability of the manufacturer and not with that imposed also to the seller of goods under Article 1730 of the Civil Code or under the Consumer's Protection Act, through the notion of contractual liability and warranty against latent defects.[165]

§1. Applicable Law

205. The delictual liability of the manufacturer vis-à-vis third parties is governed by two distinct articles of the CcQ.[166] The European Convention has been used as a source of inspiration in that respect.

§2. Regime

206. Manufacturers will be held liable in damages for the safety defect of their product. Liability also extends to the distributor and the supplier of the goods. The standard applied for the determination of the lack of safety of the product is that the manufactured good should have the quality to which a reasonable person using it is entitled. Lack of safety can result from a defect in design, in manufacturing, in preservation, or in the presentation of the goods. It can also arise from a lack of sufficient information as to the potential risks and dangers relating to its use.[167]

207. It is not clear whether the liability of the manufacturer, the distributor, and the supplier is joint and several or whether they could be held simply *in solidum*. This is, of course, particularly important where the product that has caused the damage was manufactured outside the country, leaving the plaintiff with little chance of getting compensation from it.

165. Article 1730 CcQ; and Consumer's Protection Act, RSQ, Ch. P-40.1. *See* J. Edwards 'La garantie de qualité du vendeur (En droit québécois)', 2nd edn, Montreal, Wilson and Lafleur, 2008.
166. Article 1468: 'The manufacturer of a movable property is liable to reparation for injury caused to a third person by reason of a safety defect in the thing, even if it is incorporated with or placed in an immovable for the service or operation of the immovable. The same rule applies to a person who distributes the thing under his name or as his own and to any supplier of the thing, whether a wholesaler or a retailer and whether he imported the thing.' Article 1469: 'A thing has a safety defect where, having regard to all the circumstances, it does not afford the safety which a person is normally entitled to expect, particularly by reason of a defect in the design or manufacture of the thing, poor preservation or presentation of the thing, or the lack of sufficient indications as to the risks and dangers it involves or as to safety precautions.'
167. *Baldor Electric Company v. Delisle*, 2012 QCCA 1004.

§3. Nature of Liability

208. The victim must prove the existence of the defect, the damage suffered, and the causal connection between the two. Once these facts are established, defendants, as the case may be, can still exonerate themselves in three cases.[168] Fortuitous event or act of God is the first one. Fault of the victim is the second, which implies that the victim knew or should have reasonably been aware of the defect or of the risk attached to it but, nevertheless, used the product.

209. Third, unlike other countries, Quebec has introduced the defence of technological advances. The defendant cannot be held liable if, according to the state of knowledge at the time the product was manufactured, the existence of the defect could not have been known. The risk of technological developments is thus assumed by the victim.

210. Quebec case law has not yet clearly identified the extent and nature of the delictual regime for products liability to third parties. On the one hand, it can be argued that evidence of a safety defect creates against the persons listed in Article 1468 CcQ a simple presumption of fault that can be counteracted by proof of one of the three situations mentioned earlier. On the other hand, it could also be argued that it is really a case of strict liability, since only the defect must be proven and not the fault of the manufacturer to give rise to a presumption of strict liability rebuttable only in the three different circumstances specifically provided by law.[169]

168. Article 1473 CcQ.
169. *See Baldor Electric Company v. Delisle*, 2012 QCCA 1004.

Part IV. Defences and Exemption Clauses

Chapter 1. Limitation of Action

211. The general prescriptive period that applies to cases of delictual liability is three years.[170]

212. A number of specific provisions sometimes provide for shorter or longer limitation periods. This is, oddly enough, the case for actions directed against municipalities.[171] Defamation cases[172] are also subject to a one-year prescription period that runs from the day the victim acquires knowledge of the act of defamation. Where defamation results from the publication in a newspaper, this delay is shortened to three months from either the date of publication or that of the knowledge of the victim.[173] Actions for bodily injuries resulting from a criminal offence and for damages resulting from sexual aggressions are prescribed by ten years in the first case and thirty years in the second.[174]

213. Prescription delays in tort cases like any others can be suspended[175] or interrupted.[176] Suspension exists when during the time the prescriptive period is running, the person is incapable of acting by reason of age, mental illness, or psychological incapacity. In these cases, the period will start to run again as soon as the interruptive event has disappeared.

214. Recent judgments have been rather liberal in their interpretation of Article 2904 CcQ concerning the suspension of prescription against persons who are under the impossibility to act. While under the former Code, a similar provision was interpreted to cover only absolute impossibility, courts now hold that a relative impossibility is sufficient. This applies, for example, to the victims who, because of severe

170. Article 2925 CcQ; J.-L. Baudouin, P. Deslauriers & B. Moore, *La responsabilité civile*, 8th edn, *supra*, Nos 1–1288 and ff., 1135 and ff.; and C. Gervais, *La prescription* (Cowansville: Éditions Yvon Blais, 2009).
171. Cities and Towns Act, RSQ, Ch. C-19, Art. 585.
172. Article 2929 CcQ.
173. Press Act, RSQ, Ch. P-19, Art. 2.
174. Article 2926.1 CcQ.
175. Articles 2904–2909 CcQ.
176. Articles 2889–2903 CcQ. Art. 2896 CcQ has put an end to former jurisprudential controversies and now holds that the interruption of prescription by one party produces similar effects with regard to all parties in respect to any right arising from the same source.

psychiatric disability due to the act of the tortfeasor, bring suit several years after the event occurred[177] and only when they have fully mentally recovered.

215. Finally, where the right of action results from a corporeal, moral, or material prejudice that manifests itself progressively or tardily, the prescriptive period runs from the day the damage appeared for the first time.[178] However, when the prejudice appears on a continuing basis (for instance, in the case of permanent acts of pollution), the prescription period runs from every single day that the damage is suffered.[179] The plaintiff, however, in a one action can ask both for past and future damages, as well as for an injunctive restraining order for the future.[180]

177. *Gauthier v. Beaumont* [1998], 2 SCR 3; *Auger v. Lauzon*, 2012 QCCA 27; *Catudal v. Borduas* [2006], RJQ 2052 (CA); and *Ringuette v. Ringuette* [2004], B.E. 880 (CA).
178. Article 2926 CcQ.
179. *Québec (Procureur général) v. Commission des droits de la personne et des droits de la jeunesse*, 2013 QCCA 141.
180. *Turgeon v. Dominion Tar and Chemical Co. Ltd* [1975], CA 787.

Chapter 2. Excuses and Justifications

§1. Self-defence

216. Self-defence, a classic criminal law[181] defence, is also admitted in civil cases. A person is allowed to use reasonable force to avoid damages to person or property. The standard of conduct required by civil courts, however, is less strict than that of criminal law, the rule being to determine whether the defendant, in repelling force, acted as a normally prudent and reasonable person under the circumstances.[182]

§2. Provocation

217. Provocation may also, in certain circumstances, be held to be a mitigating factor and used as a justification for imposing a division of liability between the agent and the victim.[183]

§3. Obeying Orders

218. Obeying orders is, in principle, an excuse or justification to an act that otherwise could be held to be a fault. Such is, for instance, the case of the policeman causing bodily harm while arresting a criminal. The defence of justification cannot be raised, however, if the order is illegal or if, while obeying it, the defendant commits a fault (e.g., if the policeman uses unnecessary force to perform what would otherwise be perfectly a legal arrest).[184]

§4. Consent

219. Consent of the victim can also be used as a justification provided it was free and informed. However, criminal law, as well as civil law, prohibits consent to one's death[185] with the remarkable recent exceptions under the federal and provincial statutes concerning medical aid in dying.[186]Acceptance of known risks, particularly in sporting activities, may also serve as a bar to the action or in mitigation of damages.[187]

---

181. Articles 34, 35, 37, and 234(4) Criminal Code (Cr. C.).
182. *Shank v. Morasse*, 2012 QCCQ 379; *Gignac v. Trois-Rivières (Ville de)*, 2011 QCCA 2150; and *Arseneault v. Arsenault*, 2015 QCCS 437.
183. *Hadid v. Bouhdid* [1995], RRA 469 (SC); and *Larue v. TVA Productions inc.*, 2011 QCCS 5493.
184. *Sandoli v. Communauté urbaine de Montréal* [1997], RRA 829 (SC).
185. Article 14 Cr. C.
186. An Act Respecting End of Life Care, SQ 2014 Ch. 2; and An Act to Amend the Criminal Code and Make Related Amendments to the Acts, SC 2016 C.3.
187. *See infra* para 236; *Parenteau v. SkiBromont.com* [2014] QCCS 3437; *Gagné v. Commission Scolaire de Saint-Hyacinthe* [2014] QCCS 2029; and *Mendez v. SkiBromont.com* [2013] QCCS 6256.

§5. Good Samaritan

220. The person who, acting as a good Samaritan prevents the occurrence of a prejudice to a third party, and causes damage to a third person, may be excused in cases of simple negligence under Article 1471 CcQ.[188]

188. Article 1471: 'Where a person comes to the assistance of another person or, for an unselfish motive, disposes, free of charge, of property for the benefit of another person, he is exempt from all liability for injury that may result from it, unless the injury is due to his intentional or gross fault.'

Chapter 3. Exemption Clauses

221. Exemption or exoneration clauses were held valid under the regime of the CCLC, except in cases of gross or intentional fault or negligence (*faute lourde*).[189] Courts also required that the person against whom they were raised had or could be presumed to have had actual previous knowledge of it (e.g., where a parking sign at the entrance of a parking lot was visible enough and could have easily been read).

222. With the Civil Code of 1994, this general regime was changed to afford better protection to plaintiffs. Three conditions are now imposed by law on the validity of total or partial exemption clauses. Article 1474 CcQ reads as follows:

> Art. 1474 CcQ: A person may not exclude or limit his liability for material injury caused to another through an intentional or gross fault; a gross fault is a fault which shows gross recklessness, gross carelessness or gross negligence. He may not in any way exclude or limit his liability for bodily or moral injury caused to another.

§1. Exclusion of Moral and Corporeal Damages

223. Under the new law, limitation or exclusion clauses against moral or corporeal damages are prohibited as against public order, since under Article 10 CcQ and under the Quebec Charter of Rights and Freedoms, everyone has a fundamental right to one's physical and psychological integrity.

§2. Knowledge of the Party

224. The person against whom such clauses are involved must have had previous knowledge of its terms. Where no written contract is negotiated and signed, a simple notice posted may be enough, but the party invoking it has the burden of proving that the other one was aware of its existence at the time the contract was formed. This apparently means proof of actual knowledge and not simply of presumed knowledge.

§3. Exclusion of Intentional Fault or Gross Negligence

225. Finally, no limitation or exclusion clause can be involved to cover an act of gross negligence (*faute lourde*) or an intentional fault. The exact definition of gross negligence (*faute lourde*) has been left to the courts to decide. It is, generally speaking, an act or omission that shows a total and wanton disregard for the rights of others and is close to criminal negligence.[190]

---

189. *Furness, Withy and Co. Ltd v. Vipand* [1971], SCR 54: 521.

190. *Télémontage Inc. v. Air Canada* [1981], CA 146; and *Audet v. Transamerica Life Canada*, 2012 QCCA 1746.

§4. RESTRICTIVE INTERPRETATION

226. Finally, the tradition of the Quebec jurisprudence has been to apply to these clauses the contra proferentem, rule of interpretation, against the person invoking it. Moreover, in contractual matters, Article 1435 CcQ concerning consumers or adhesion contracts and external clauses as well as Article 1436 CcQ dealing with illegible or incomprehensible clauses also afford, for those two types of contracts, an added protection against possible abuses.

Part V. Causation

Chapter 1. Concept

§1. Identification

227. The identification of an adequate causal connection between the fault of the defendant and the loss suffered by the plaintiff is not an easy task, because it is not simply a legal problem but also and mostly a philosophical one.

228. Authors have written extensively on this topic, both in the context of civil liability and in that of criminal law.[191]

229. Quebec courts have approached the problem of causation from a strictly practical point of view and have repeatedly refused to take part in doctrinal controversies and abstract discussions on the subject. They have refused to adopt as such the various doctrines of the equivalence of conditions, immediate causation, and proximate cause. They rely mostly on the theory of adequate causation, coupled sometimes, with the reasonable expectation test. They follow a general tendency to treat and analyse the problem as a purely factual one, without feeling the necessity of justifying their solution by theoretical considerations.[192]

230. In medical malpractice cases, the equivalence of conditions theory is however applied when the physician has not adequately informed the patient of the potential risks of the medical act. The physician, even if no medical or technical act of negligence exists, will be held liable for the occurrence of the risks that the patient had not been informed of. In such cases, the causal connection between the damages and the original fault is really weak, and the non-compliance of the duty to obtain free and informed consent is really more the occasion than the real cause of the prejudice suffered.[193]

---

191. J.-L. Baudouin, P. Deslauriers & B. Moore, *La responsabilité civile*, 8th edn, *supra*, Nos 1–663 and ff., 709 and ff.
192. *See Benhaim v. St Germain*, 2016 CSC 48.
193. R. Kouri and S. Philips-Nootens, 'L'intégrité de la personne et le consentement aux soins', 4e edn., Cowansville, Éditions Yvon Blais, 2017; R. Kouri, 'L'obligation de renseignement en matière de responsabilité médicale et la subjectivité rationnelle: mariage de convenance ou mésalliance?', RDUS 24 (1994): 345; and L. Khoury, *Uncertain Causation in Medical Liability* (Cowansville: Éditions Yvon Blais, 2006).

231. In medical and malpractice cases, the Supreme Court has repeatedly underlined the difference between scientific causation (which has a complete or high degree of certainty) and legal causation. In the latter case, plaintiff only needs to discharge the burden of proving causation according to the ordinary test of the balance of probabilities.[194] The Supreme Court also recently held that courts may, but are by no means obliged to, draw a presumption of causation when the defendant by his or her own act has compromised the possibility for the plaintiff to prove effective causation.[195]

§2. JURISPRUDENTIAL CRITERIA

232. By and large, courts require that the damage be the direct, logical, and immediate consequence of the fault. Indirect damages are thus excluded by separating the real and actual cause of the damage from the mere circumstances or occasions that helped create it. The reasonable expectation test is also frequently used in that respect. Did the factual circumstances make it probable for a reasonable person to expect the realization of the damage? Should the answer be positive, causality is deemed to be proven.

§3. *NOVUS ACTUS INTERVENIENS*

233. Difficulties arise with the interruption of the causal connection between the original fault and the damage, due to the intervention of a *novus actus*, which can be either the subsequent fault of a third party, the fault of the victim, or the occurrence of a fortuitous event.

234. In the first and second hypotheses, the author of the first act of negligence will be totally exonerated if the degree of fault of the second tortfeasor or of the victim is higher.[196] In certain cases, the situation will resolve itself by a split responsibility verdict between the two.[197] If the *novus actus interveniens* is a fortuitous event or an act of God, in strict logic, the solution should be that the author of the original act of negligence be totally exonerated. However, some cases, probably for reasons of equity, and to ensure that the victim is not left without any form of compensation, have retained the responsibility of the first agent.

235. As a general rule, the burden of proof of causation rests on the plaintiff. However, the plaintiff can, in a number of cases, benefit from presumptions created by law that will make it easier for him or her to discharge it. Presumptions of fact

---

194. *Snell v. Farrell*, [1990] 2 RCS 311; *St-Jean v. Mercier*, [2002] 1 RCS 491; and *Benhaim v. St Germain*, 2016 CSC 48.
195. *Benhaim v. St Germain*, 2016 CSC 48.
196. *Pourvoirie de l'Ours brun Inc. v. Tremblay* [1997], RRA 692 (CA).
197. *Deguire Avenue Ltd v. Adler* [1963], KB 101.

also play an important role in that respect.[198] Also, where the plaintiff can demonstrate that, as a general rule, damage identical to that suffered does occur where the same type of fault is committed, causation is held to be conclusively proven.

198. Articles 2846 and ff. CcQ; *Biondi v. Montréal (Ville de)*; 2013 QCCA 404, 2013, 3 SCR 949.

Chapter 2. Contribution to Damages

236. Problems related to the apportionment of damages between various persons relate directly to the identification of causality. Damage can result from a combination of different acts and of several factors that may, in certain circumstances, act as mitigation of the global prejudice caused.

§1. Fault of the Victim and of a Third Party

237. This first case occurs where the damage is the result of a combination of two faults: one by a third party and the other by the victim. In such case, the plaintiff can only recover that portion of the total damage that is directly related to the fault of the third party and must assume the economic consequences of his or her own fault.[199] Article 1479 CcQ codifies the long-standing rule that the victim must take all reasonable means to minimize his or her losses.

238. Courts have often applied (especially in relation to the practice of sports) the principle *volenti non fit injuria*, according to which victims must assume the normal consequences of exposing themselves to dangerous activities and cannot recover, should that risk occur, unless it could not have been reasonably foreseen and the victim willingly accepted it.[200]

239. Quebec courts have always refused to apply the common law doctrine of contributory negligence, according to which victims cannot claim any compensation if their fault had contributed in any degree to the creation of the damage. Under Article 1478 CcQ, when the damage is caused by the fault of the victim and that of a third party, liability is thus shared in proportion to the degree of the fault of each party.

§2. Faults of Several Third Parties

240. A second hypothesis is where the damage is related to a combination of different actions by a number of third parties.

I. Common Fault

241. The first possibility is where several individuals engage together in a single act that causes the whole damage. In this case of common fault, the victim, under

199. Article 1478 CcQ; and J.-L. Baudouin, P. Deslauriers & B. Moore, *La responsabilité civile*, 8th edn, *supra*, Nos 1–708 and ff., 736 and ff.
200. L. Giroux, 'L'acceptation des risques', *C. de D.* 9 (1968): 65; *Corbeil v. Mont St-Sauveur International*, 2013 QCCS 1561; *Arasimowicz v. Montréal (Ville de)*, 2012 QCCS 526; *Girard v. Ville de Baie-Comeau*, 2016 QCCS 6541; and *Dionne v. Fortin*, 2016 QCCQ 15502.

Article 1526 CcQ can sue one or the other of the several tortfeasors, who are held jointly and severally liable. Between them, the responsibility is, in principle, shared equally unless there is proof to the contrary.

II. Contributory Fault

242. A second possibility is that of contributory fault, where two or more acts of negligence, this time distinct and separate one from another, have caused only one global prejudice. The victim can then claim the whole of the damages suffered from both or from one of the tortfeasors. Their respective shares of responsibility will not, however, necessarily be of equal proportion.

III. Successive Faults

243. A third possibility is that of successive faults, where several acts of negligence have contributed to the damage but were executed at different times and in succession one to another. Liability cannot then be joint and several, and the victim must attempt to recover from each of the agents their shares of the total damage related to each fault.

IV. Simultaneous Faults

244. The next case is that of simultaneous faults. Like the previous one, several acts of negligence are executed separately, but it is however impossible to determine which part of the global damage can be attributed to a particular act.[201] This situation causes difficulties for the victim who runs the risk (because of the impossibility of proving which part of the total damage is related to each act) to lose successively each and every one of the defendants. Article 1480 CcQ codifies[202] a solution devised earlier by case law: when such determination is impossible, the tortfeasors are held jointly and severally liable.

§3. Exoneration under the Law

245. Under Article 1481 CcQ, where the damage has been caused by several persons but one of them is exempted from liability by a specific provision of the law, his or her share of liability is equally divided among the others.

---

201. A. Mayrand, 'L'énigme des fautes simultanées', *R. du B.* 18 (1958): 1.

202. Article 1480: 'Where several persons have jointly taken part in a wrongful act which has resulted in injury or have committed separate faults each of which may have caused the injury, and where it is impossible to determine, in either case, which of them actually caused it, they are solidarity liable for reparation thereof.'

§4. FAULT AND FORTUITOUS EVENT

246. Finally, where the damage has been caused in part by the fault of a third party and in part by a fortuitous event, as we have already seen, the third party is only accountable for the proportion of the whole damage that is directly connected to his or her fault.

Part VI. Remedies

247. The existence of a damage causing a loss or harm is the third general condition to civil liability. An act of gross negligence that is without consequences will not trigger civil liability. The damage suffered by the victim is, as a general rule, usually compensated by a monetary award, but will sometimes also give rise to other remedies. Injunctions, for example, can be granted to prevent the occurrence of foreseeable harm or stop its continuation.[203]

203. P.-A. Gendreau & Al, *L'injonction* (Cowansville: Éditions Yvon Blais, 1998).

Chapter 1. General Principles

248. Damages awards by courts must meet certain conditions.

§1. Criteria

I. Directness

249. Not all damages suffered by the defendant are open to compensation. The law restricts compensation only to those losses that have a direct causal relation to the fault, and Article 1607 CcQ[204] codifies the well-accepted rule that only direct damages can be compensated. Those that qualify as too remote are excluded. The identification of direct damages has given rise to a number of problems in Quebec jurisprudence,[205] because of the inherent difficulty to clearly identify them. It is now well settled, however, that direct damages concern not only those caused to the immediate victim, but also those suffered by third parties resulting from the same negligent act. For instance, courts have repeatedly held valid the claim for loss of *consortium* and *servitium* of a spouse whose consort has been injured.[206]

250. In a similar way, courts have also compensated family members for nervous shock suffered by them as a result of an accident caused to another member of the family.[207]

251. It is also now settled law that the insurer, under a liability insurance policy, who has paid off his or her insured client, can sue the tortfeasor directly (Article 2474 CcQ). Article 2501 CcQ also gives the option to the victim to sue directly the insured or the insurer, or both of them in the same action, thus ending a conflicting line of case law under the CCLC.

252. Expert fees incurred in court to prove the loss suffered are also generally considered to be direct damages.[208] Lawyer's fees, however, were held for a long time not to be recoverable. Recent cases, however, have created an exception to that rule. Lawyer's fees incurred to defend against a false criminal accusation, or a clearly abusive procedure, can be claimed as direct damages.[209]

---

204. Article 1607 CcQ: 'The creditor is entitled to damages for bodily, moral or material injury which is an immediate and direct consequence of the debtor's default.' *See* J.-L. Baudouin, P. Deslauriers & B. Moore, *La responsabilité civile*, 8th edn, *supra*, Nos 1–319 and ff., 363 and ff.
205. *Congrégation des petits frères de Marie v. Regent Taxi and Transport Co.*[1929], SCR 650.
206. *Lister v. McAnnulty* [1944], SCR 317; and *Cazes v. Pohénégamook (Ville de)*, 2012 QCCS 2836.
207. *Rousseau v. Quessy* [1986], RRA 222 (SC); and *Stephanik v. Hôpital Hôtel-Dieu* [1997], RJQ 1332 (SC).
208. *Hôpital Notre-Dame de l'Espérance v. Laurent* [1978], 1 SCR 605; *Association des professeurs de Lignery v. Comeau* [1990], RJQ 130 (CA); and *Maison Simons inc. v. Lizotte*, 2010 QCCA 2126.
209. *Boulianne v. Commission des écoles catholiques de Québec* [1997], RJQ 2792 (SC); *Charlebois v. Derome* [1998], RRA 235 (SC); *Vallée de la Gatineau (Municipalité régionale de la) v. Charron*, 2013 QCCQ 4616; and *Agence du revenu du Québec v. Groupe Enico inc.*, 2016 QCCA 76.

II. Certainty

253. The second condition is that the damage suffered must be certain, requiring the plaintiff to prove that it has already occurred or that it will occur in the future. Certainty is not, however, an absolute concept, and courts only require that the occurrence of the damage be reasonably certain under the circumstances. Such is the case for compensation of future physical incapacity. Medical expert evidence will help to determine the probability of future adverse effects and evaluate the degree of seriousness of future physical or mental incapacity to help determine a global monetary award.

254. Compensation for the loss of a chance has, like the situation in French civil law, given rise to jurisprudential controversies in legal and professional malpractice cases.[210] Clients will be compensated for loss if, due to the fault of the lawyer, they have lost the possibility of bringing a potentially victorious claim before the courts. The determining factor for the courts will be the probability of success of the legal proceedings. In medical cases, patients will also be compensated if, according to the balance of probabilities, the act or omission of the physician has brought about the loss of the possibility to recover one's health. Expert evidence must, of course, clearly show the probability that the patient would really have had a chance to recover and be cured.

255. Another problem recently raised before the courts concerns the possibility of claiming as direct damages in addition to the legal court costs the lawyer's fees incurred by the plaintiffs. Courts will now grant them where the behaviour of the other party shows bad faith or gross negligence, in other words, when the judicial process has abused.[211] Amendments to the new Code of Civil Procedure do grant a large discretionary power to the courts.[212]

III. Lawfulness

256. Damage suffered during the course of an illicit activity cannot be compensated.[213] The same rule applies to situations where under the general principles of civil law because an award would be considered to offend public order. For instance, Quebec courts have dismissed claims for wrongful life brought by a child for having been born, despite the fact that his or her parents had undertaken sterilization procedures. Courts based their decision on the principle that life, in itself, cannot be

210. *Laferrière v. Lawson* [1991], 1 SCR 541. See S. Nootens, 'La perte de chance', *R. du B.* 50 (1990): 611; and S. Gaudet, 'La perte de chance: un miroir aux alouettes', in *Mélanges Jean Pineau* (Montréal: Éditions Thémis, 2003), 186.

211. *Coopérative d'habitation Jeanne-Mance v. Choueke*, [2001] RJQ 1441 (CA); *Viel v. Entreprises immobilières du terroir Ltée.*, [2002] RJQ 1262 (CA).

212. Articles 51 and ff. CCP.

213. *Gourd v. Simard* [1979], CA 272.

said to be a damage.[214] They have, however, in similar circumstances compensated the parents for the additional financial burden caused by birth of the unwanted child.[215]

§2. FUNCTIONS

257. The function of pecuniary damage compensation are threefold. First, it must compensate the effective loss suffered by the victim. Second, it must include all of the direct damages and put, as much as possible, the victims back in the same position they would have been, had the delict not been committed. Third, the compensation must be awarded once and for all.

I. Compensation for Effective Loss

258. Compensation includes two basic elements. Under Article 1611 CcQ, it must make up for the actual loss suffered as well as for the profit the victim has been deprived of. The process of judicial assessment is relatively simple, where damages to property or economic damages are involved, but becomes much more difficult where non-pecuniary or 'moral' damages are concerned. What, for instance, should be a reasonable compensation for the non-pecuniary loss resulting from invasion of privacy or defamation?

259. Punitive damages constitute an exception to this rule. These are well known in Anglo-American common law and were not, in the past, part of the tradition of Quebec civil law, except in cases provided for by a limited number of very specific statutes.[216] The scope has significantly increased with the adoption in the 1970s of the *Quebec Charter of Rights and Freedoms*,[217] which specifically allows for punitive damages in cases of violations of a right protected by the Charter when it results both from an illicit and intentional act.[218]

260. A Supreme Court decision has attempted to define more specifically the term 'intentional'. According to the *St. Ferdinand* case,[219] it is now well settled that it requires wilful intent on the part of the tortfeasor and that gross negligence or wanton disregard of the rights of others is simply not sufficient. The act must be a deliberate one.

214. *Suite v. Cook* [1995], RJQ 2765 (CA).
215. *Cataford v. Moreau* [1978], SC 933; and *Engstrom v. Courteau* [1986], RJQ 3048 (SC).
216. J.-L. Baudouin, P. Deslauriers & B. Moore, *La responsabilité civile*, 8th edn, *supra*, Nos 1–373. and ff. 411 and ff.
217. Quebec Charter of Rights and Freedoms, RSQ, Ch. C-12, Art. 49.
218. C. Dallaire, *La mise en œuvre des dommages exemplaires sous le régime des chartes*, 2nd edn (Montreal: Wilson et Lafleur).
219. *Curateur public v. Syndicat national de l'Hôpital St-Ferdinand* [1996], 3 SCR 211.

261. The CcQ still lacks a general provision allowing for punitive damages. Only a very few number of specific articles and statutes now make them available in particular circumstances.[220]

262. By and large, courts have followed the criteria set forth in Article 1621 CcQ in their evaluation of punitive damages – i.e., the seriousness of the fault; the financial situation of the defendant; and the extent of reparation for which defendant has already been held liable for. The amounts granted by the courts in Quebec are substantially lower than those awarded by the United States or other Canadian courts,[221] although they have increased in recent years.[222]

II. Full Compensation

263. The basic principle is that of restitutio in integrum, which means that the amount must be such as to put victims in the same financial position as they would have been if the accident had not occurred. The problem is relatively simple where the damage is caused to a thing or property. The commercial or replacement value is usually the measure of the loss suffered. It is more problematic in cases involving personal injury or wrongful death.

264. Quebec courts, following the common law doctrine of the 'thin skull rule', do take into consideration the previous state of health of the victim, and the defendant must assume the risks of the individual state of health of the victim.

265. In certain cases, compensation for the harm caused may be totally or partially obtained from another source than the defendant. Such is the case where indemnities are paid through social security or state insurance schemes. In that respect, courts have held that, because the victim contributed financially to these programmes by paying taxes, the amounts thus collected cannot be deducted from the amount of indemnity that the defendant has to pay, or taken into consideration in evaluating it in the absence of a specific legal provision to the contrary. The same solution applies to payments under insurance policies held by the victim. Under Article 1608 CcQ,[223] compensation by the defendant cannot be reduced or altered by the fact that the victim has received payments from a third party. This also holds true for voluntary payments made to the victim by the employer.[224]

220. For example, Arts 1988, 1902, and 1968 CcQ.

221. *See*, however, the recent decision of *Thériault-Martel v. Savoie* [2014] QCCS 3937 (in appeal).

222. *See*, however, *Ville de Sainte-Marthe-sur-le-Lac v. Expert-conseils RB inc., 2017 QCCA 381; Agence du revenu du Québec v. Groupe Enico inc.*, 2016 QCCA 76; and *Savoie v. Thériault-Martel*, 2015 QCCA 591.

223. Article 1608: 'The obligation of the debtor to pay damages to the creditor is neither reduced nor altered by the fact that the creditor receives a prestation from a third person, as a result of the injury he has sustained, except so far as the third person is subrogated to the rights of the creditor.'

224. J.-L. Baudouin, P. Deslauriers & B. Moore, *La responsabilité civile*, 8th edn, *supra*, Nos 1–422 and ff., 469 and ff.

III. Final Compensation

266. Unlike the system known in most European countries, compensation is paid once and for all in one lump sum of capital and not spread out in annuity payments, with two exceptions. Under Article 1616 CcQ, where bodily injuries have been suffered by a minor child, the Court can order payment in whole or in part under the form of an annuity. Within three months after reaching the age of majority, the victim can demand immediate payment of the capital amount still owing.

267. Under Article 1615 CcQ, also exclusively in cases of personal injuries, the court may, for a period not exceeding three years, reserve the right of the victims to apply for additional compensation if, at the time of trial, their exact physical condition is impossible to determine with sufficient accuracy.[225]

268. If the situation of the victim changes before the end of the trial, the parties can amend their claims at any time before final judgment to reflect changes in the situation of the victim during this period. Should, for instance, the victim die during trial, the heirs can act in continuance of suit, and the Court will consider that fact in the calculation of the amount owed.

269. Should the situation of the victim change between the trial judgment and the appeal decision, Article 363 of the Code of Civil Procedure gives discretion to the CA to allow new evidence that might have a bearing on the amount of damages that should, in all fairness, be awarded.

225. *Rocheleau v. Métabetchouan-Lac-à-la-Croix (Municipalité de)*, 2012 QCCQ 6729; and *Gravel v. Lifesitenews.com (Canada)*, 2013 QCCS 36.

Chapter 2. Compensation for Damages: Specific Awards

§1. Compensation for Damages to Property

270. Compensation for property or material damages is relatively easy to assess and takes into account both the actual loss suffered and the gain the victim has been deprived of.

271. Generally speaking, the objective market or commercial value of the goods remains the classical basis of evaluation. If the object is totally destroyed or rendered useless, a sum representing the free market value, less depreciation, is the rule, unless the debtor shows that it does not correspond to a fair economic or personal value. If the object has only been damaged, but can still be used, compensation will include the costs of repair, all direct and necessary expenses incurred by the victim in that respect, as well as a sum for the loss of enjoyment of the property.

§2. Compensation for Bodily Injuries

I. General Rules

272. A series of important Supreme Court decisions in 1978 have set the basic ground rules for the compensation of bodily injuries throughout Canada.[226] Courts must follow three fundamental principles. First, the evaluation must be a detailed one. An award lumping together all the different heads of damages is no longer acceptable. Second, the indemnity must be calculated according to an acceptable actuarial method, taking into account capital depreciation, discount rules, interest rates, fiscal impact, etc. Third, the award must compensate once and for all for both present and future damages.

II. Physical Incapacity

273. The degree of physical or mental incapacity, both present and future, is determined by courts according to expert evidence. Incapacity can be temporary or permanent, total, or partial. Courts, having agreed upon a percentage of incapacity, will then take into consideration the life expectancy of the victim and the discount rate (i.e., the difference between the inflation rate and the rate of interest on a capital investment) to arrive at a global capital sum that, invested under normal conditions, should compensate the victim each year during his or her normal life expectancy for the loss suffered.

---

226. *Andrews v. Grand and Toy Alberta Ltd* [1978], 2 SCR 229; *Thorton v. Board of School Trustees of School District No 57* [1978], 2 SCR 267; *Arnold v. Teno* [1978], 2 SCR 237; and *Keizer v. Hanna* [1978], 2 SCR 342. *See also* D. Gardner, *L'évaluation du préjudice corporel*, 4th edn (Cowansville: Éditions Yvon Blais, 2016).

274. Final compensation will also include all necessary expenses related to health care (medical, pharmaceutical, nursing care, etc.) not already covered by Medicare. In that respect, the Supreme Court has made it very clear that victims of permanent and severe injuries have the option of either staying in a hospital or specialized home or of returning home. Should they choose the latter option, all expenses incurred to adapt their house to the new situation are recoverable as direct damages, as well as those necessary, as the case may be, to buy and replace a car adapted to the specific physical handicap.[227]

III. Economic Loss

275. Compensation also includes loss of future revenues. Courts will take into consideration the economic impact for the victim of the accident. The loss of economic capacity to generate financial gains is, of course, a direct damage. The evaluation of economic loss is relatively easy if the victim, before the accident, had a stable profession or employment. Courts then, according to the life and employment expectancy of the victim, will take into consideration future increases in salaries and future promotions that he or she would normally have benefited from to determine the award.

276. This assessment is more difficult particularly in the case of women where the victim, after marriage, has decided to abandon work and to stay home and raise a family. Up to now, courts have not yet found a scientific and truly satisfactory system of compensation. They do take into consideration the possibility that the victim would, in the future, have returned to a profitable job or profession. If there is no such indication, a nominal sum will usually be awarded.

277. Problems also arise where young children are concerned. If the child already has had an educational background, some objective basis can then be found to determine the loss, because there may exist elements pointing to the kind of employment the child would have held under normal circumstances. This is not, however, the case with infants, and courts usually take, as a basis, the average remuneration of the Quebec worker.

IV. Non-economic Loss

278. Finally, the courts will compensate the victim for what is called non-economic loss – i.e., the loss of amenities of life, pain and suffering, loss of enjoyment of life, and aesthetic prejudice. By and large, these sums are still, in Quebec, relatively modest as compared to those awarded by American courts.

227. *Thorton v. Board of School Trustees of School District No 57* [1978], 2 SCR 267.

§3. COMPENSATION FOR WRONGFUL DEATH

279. Two different remedies are available in cases of wrongful death.

I. Action by the Heirs

280. First, an action in damages can be brought by the heirs of the victim to cover the loss suffered by the victim between the time of the accident and the time of death. Compensation will include, as the case may be loss of financial gains or salary, a sum for temporary physical incapacity, reimbursement of expenses, and an indemnity for pain and suffering. In other words, the heirs will claim the damages that would have been due anyway to the victim up to the time of death. Courts have, however, refused to allow a claim by the heirs for loss of future benefits that they could have derived from the succession had the victim lived a longer life, for two reasons. First, the damage is not certain, because absolute freedom of will is the rule under Quebec law. Second, the damage is really impossible to assess.[228]

281. For pain and suffering, two conditions are required. First, victims must have lived to be conscious of their physical or mental pain. The heirs of a person who died after spending some time in a deep comatose state have been denied compensation.[229] Second, the time between the accident and the death of the victim must have been sufficiently long to allow for experiencing pain. Thus, sudden death does not give rise to compensation.[230]

II. Direct Action

282. The second type of action resulting from wrongful death is the direct action taken by those persons who, related or not related to the victims, have suffered a personal loss by reason of their death. In that respect, the CcQ has finally done away with former Article 1056 CCLC, which restricted this recourse only to married consorts, ascendants, and descendants.

283. Under the new Civil Code, any person can validly claim, provided the damage caused is certain and direct. Most of the time, plaintiffs will be close relatives (consorts, children, or parents), but nothing prevents the demand of an unrelated person (e.g., an associate and an employer).

284. Damages that can be claimed under the direct action are of two types: moral and economic. Moral or non-pecuniary damages, also known as *solatium doloris*, attempt to compensate the plaintiffs for the moral pain and the suffering they have experienced as a result of the accidental death of the victim. This type of

228. *Pantel v. Air Canada* [1975], 1 SCR 472.
229. *Covet v. Jewish General Hospital* [1976], SC 1390.
230. *Driver v. Coca Cola Ltd* [1961], SCR 201.

damages can now be claimed before the Quebec courts, as a result of a Supreme Court decision that overruled a former one prohibiting such award.[231]

285. Economic damages include all those representing the actual and potential financial losses of the plaintiff resulting from the death of the victim. The calculation is a complex one. Consorts will claim for the loss of actual or potential financial support, so will children for the loss of a mother or father. Courts, to arrive at a fair amount, take into consideration a number of different factors, such as the age of the victim and of the claimants, their life expectancy, the profession or job held by the victim at the time of his or her death, and the reasonable expectancy of potential financial support. By and large, Quebec courts have not been very generous in that respect, and these awards remain somewhat modest. Loss of moral or intellectual support also gives rise to compensation.[232]

231. *See supra* para. 5.
232. *See* D. Gardner, 'L'évaluation du préjudice corporel', 4d edn (Cowansville, Éditions Yvon Blais, 2016).

General Conclusion

286. Other areas of Quebec law of civil responsibility that are important could not be developed in the current monograph because of length limitations. The present monograph attempts only to give a general idea of the Quebec regime. This is the case, for example, with the legislation concerning industrial accidents.[233] Workers injured, as well as their dependants, can claim from an independent administrative board for damages incurred during the performance of the work or at the occasion of its performance.[234] In such cases, as a general rule, no recourse can be brought by the worker before the regular courts. In a limited number of situations, however (e.g., where part of the damage was caused by a third party), an option is still open to get either the predetermined compensation from the Board or to sue before the regular courts for the actual amount of damages suffered.

287. This is also the case for victims of criminal acts[235] and for damage suffered in the performance of acts of good citizenship.[236] Two sets of legislation provide for compensation for loss suffered by the victim of a crime or by the person who, acting as a good citizen, has helped others and suffered a prejudice by reason thereof.

288. The reader will, however, find here a short Selected Bibliography that will help in providing a more detailed view of these areas, as well as of those summarily covered in this document.

289. The civil law system of delictual liability in Quebec is, at least at the level of general principles, comparable to that of other civilian countries such as France; indeed, both doctrinal works and French jurisprudence are of importance for Quebec and often cited by the courts. Yet, it has undeniably been influenced in certain aspects by the Anglo-American tradition.

290. A comparison between the Quebec law of civil liability and the Canadian common law system of torts clearly shows that, in spite of a different theoretical

233. *An Act Respecting Industrial Accidents and Occupational Diseases*, RSQ, Ch. A-3.001.
234. B. Cliche, S. Lafontaine, & R. Mailhot, *Traité de droit de la santé et de la sécurité au travail: le régime juridique de la prévention des accidents du travail et des maladies professionnelles* (Cowansville: Éditions Yvon Blais, 1997); and L. Corriveau, *Les accidents du travail* (Cowansville: Éditions Yvon Blais, 1991).
235. *An Act Respecting Assistance for Victims of Crime*, RSQ, Ch. A-13.2.
236. *An Act to Promote Good Citizenship*, RSQ, Ch. C-20.

and intellectual approach to the analysis of legal problems and a different classification and qualification of topics, the general results and solutions arrived at by the courts are, if not totally identical, very similar one to the other. The real differences lie much more in both analytical and reasoning processes.

Selected Bibliography

The Quebec case law and doctrinal works are numerous. The present bibliography is restricted only to the main sources.

§1. Books: Civil Liability in General

Baudouin, J.-L., P. Deslauriers, & Moore, B. *La responsabilité civile*. 8th edn. Cowansville: Éditions Yvon Blais, 2014.
Gardner, D. *L'évaluation du préjudice corporel*. 4th edn. Cowansville: Éditions Yvon Blais, 2016.
Juriclasseur. *Obligations et responsabilité*. LexisNexis, 2009, civile 7; Collection de droit du Barreau, 2009–2010, vol. 4.
Karim, V. *Les Obligations*. 4th edn. Vol. I. Cowansville: Éditions Yvon Blais, 2015.
Lévesque, F., *Précis de droit québécois des obligations,* Cowansville: Éditions Yvon Blais, 2014.
Masse, C. 'La responsabilité civile'. In *La réforme du Code civil*. Vol. II. Québec: Presses de l'Université Laval, 1993.
Nadeau, A. & R. Nadeau. *Traité pratique de responsabilité civile*. Montréal: Wilson et Lafleur, 1971.
Perret, L. *Précis de responsabilité civile*. Ottawa: Éditions de l'Université d'Ottawa, 1979.
Philips-Nootens, S., P. Lesage-Jarjoura & R. Kouri. *Éléments de responsabilité civile médicale*. 4th edn. Cowansville: Éditions Yvon Blais, 20016.
Pineau, J., D. Burman & S. Gaudet. *Théorie des obligations*. 4th edn. Montréal: Éditions Thémis, 2001.
Pineau, J. & M. Ouellette. *Théorie de la responsabilité civile*. Montréal: Éditions Thémis, 1980.
Tancelin, M. *Des obligations: en droit mixte du Québec*. 7th edn. Montréal: Wilson & Lafleur, 2009.

§2. Scope of Delictual Liability

Crépeau, P.-A. 'Des régimes contractuel et délictuel de la responsabilité civile en droit canadien'. *McGill L.J.* 22 (1962): 501.
Crépeau, P.-A. 'Le contenu obligationnel d'un contrat'. CBR 43 (1965): I.

Crépeau, P.-A. 'L'indemnisation de la victime par ricochet d'un accident mortel résultant de l'inexécution d'un devoir contractuel'. *McGill L.J.* 26 (1982): 567.
Deslauriers, P. 'Droit québécois et droit français des obligations: divergence et concordance'. In *Droit québécois et droit français: communauté, autonomie, concordance*. Cowansville: Éditions Yvon Blais, 1992.
Gardner, D. & B. Moore. 'La responsabilité contractuelle dans la tourmente'. *C. de D.* 48 (2007): 543.
Gaudet, S. & J. Pineau. '*La responsabilité légale: face cachée de la responsabilité extracontactuelle* in *Mélanges Jean-Louis Baudouin*'. Cowansville: Éditions Yvon Blais, 2012: 751.
Jobin, P.G. 'Amputer la responsabilité contractuelle? Une tourmente inutile et néfaste'. *C. de D.* 50 (2009): 3.
Viney, G. 'Pour une interpretation modérée et raisonnée du refus d'option entre responsabilité contractuelle et responsabilité délictuelle'. *McGill L.J.* 39 (1994): 813.
Zhou, H.R. 'Le test de la personne raisonnable en responsabilité civile'. *R. du B* 61 (2006): 453.

§3. Fault and Capacity

Chevrette, C., & P. Collins Hoffman. 'Responsabilité des administrateurs de société par actions au Québec'. Cowansville: Éditions Yvon Blais, 2016.
Daoust, C. & L. Verschelden. 'Le droit québécois de la responsabilité civile des syndicats en cas de grève illegale'. *Montréal, École des relations industrielles*, 1980.
Flannigan, R. 'The Personal Tort Liability of Directors'. *R. du B. Can.* 81 (2002): 247.
Haanappel, P. 'Faute et risque dans le système québécois de la responsabilité civile extracontractuelle'. *McGill L.J.* 24 (1978): 635.
Jobin, P. 'La violation d'une loi ou d'un règlement entraîne-t-elle la responsabilité civile?'. *R. du B. Can.* 44 (1984): 222.
Kasirer, N. 'The Infans as Bon Père de Famille: Objectively Wrongful Conduct in the Civil Law Tradition'. *Am. J. Comp. L.* 40 (1992): 343.
Lacroix, M. *L'illicéité: essai théorique et comparatif en matière de responsabilité civile extracontractuelle pour le fait personnel*. Cowansville: Éditions Yvon Blais, 2013.
Martel, P. *Devoirs et responsabilités des administrateurs de corporations sans but lucratif au Québec*. Montréal: Wilson & Lafleur, 1990.
Martel, P. 'Le voile corporatif et l'article 317 du Code civil'. *R. du B.* 55 (1995): 497.
Trudel, P. 'La faute journalistique en droit civil'. *R.J.T.* 49 (2015): 637.

§4. MEDICAL MALPRACTICE

Baudouin, J.-L. 'La responsabilité professionnelle médicale: pathologie et thérapie'. In *La responsabilité civile des professionnels au Canada*. Cowansville: Éditions Yvon Blais, 1988.
Bernardot, A. & R. Kouri. *La responsabilité civile médicale*. Sherbrooke: Éditions Revue de Droit, 1980.
Bernardot, A. & R. Kouri. 'La responsabilité du centre hospitalier et du fabricant résultant du fait d'appareils médicaux défectueux'. *McGill L.J.* 26 (1981): 976.
Bourgoignie, T. (ed.). *Accidents thérapeutiques et protection du consommateur*. Cowansville: Éditions Yvon Blais, 2006.
Chalifoux, D. 'Vers une nouvelle relation commettant-préposé'. *R. du B.* 44 (1984): 815.
Chénier, R.J. 'Resource, Allocation and the Standard of Care of Physicians'. CBR 83 (2004): 1.
Crépeau, P.-A. 'La responsabilité civile de l'établissement hospitalier'. *McGill L.J.* 26 (1981): 673.
De la Sablonnière, L. & Paquet M.-N. 'La responsabilité hospitalière et l'utilisation du matériel'. In *Développements récents en droit medico-légal*, Cowansville: Éditions Yvon Blais, 2011: 101.
Deleury, É. and Goubau, D. 'Le droit des personnes physiques'. 5th edn. Cowansville: Éditions Yvons Blais, 2014.
Goldberg, R., 'Epidemiological Uncertainty, Causation and Drug Product Liability'. *Mc Gill L.J.* 59 (2014): 777.
Khoury, L. *Uncertain Causation in Medical Liability*. Cowansville: Éditions Yvon Blais, 2006.
Khoury, L. 'Faute, responsabilité individuelle et médecine moderne'. In *Mélanges Jean-Louis Baudouin*, Cowansville: Éditions Yvon Blais, 2012: 773.
Khoury, L. 'Le juge canadien, anglais et australien devant l'incertitude causale en matière de responsabilité médicale'. *Mc Gill L.J.* 43 (2014): 989.
Kouri, R. 'La causalité et l'obligation en droit médical québécois'. RDUS 17 (1987): 493.
Kouri, R. 'L'obligation de renseignement en matière de responsabilité médicale et la subjectivité rationnelle: mariage de convenance ou mésalliance?'. RDUS 24 (1994): 345.
Kouri, R. 'From Presumptions of Fact to Presumptions of Causation: Reflections on the Perils of Judge-Made Rules in Quebec Medical Malpractice Law'. RDUS 32 (2001): 213.
Kouri, R. & S. Nootens. 'L'expérimentation et les soins innovateurs: l'article 21 CcQ et les affres de l'imprécision'. RDUS 27 (1997): 89.
Kouri, R. & S. Nootens. *L'intégrité de la personne et le consentement aux soins*. 3rd edn. Cowansville: Éditions Yvon Blais, 2012.
Lajoie, A., P. Molinari, & J.-L. Baudouin. 'Le droit aux services de santé: légal ou contractuel?' *R. du B.* 43 (1984): 675.
Letendre, M. 'Le devoir du médecin de prévenir les membres de la famille d'un patient atteint d'une maladie génétique'. *McGill L.J.* 49 (2004): 555.

Ménard, J.P. 'L'obligation de suivre'. In *Développements récents en droit medico-légal*, Cowansville: Éditions Yvon Blais, 2011: 123.
Ménard, J.P. & D. Martin. *La responsabilité médicale pour la faute d'autrui*. Cowansville: Éditions Yvon Blais, 1992.
Morissette, Y. & D. Shuman. 'Le secret professionnel au Québec: un hydre à trenteneuf têtes rôde dans le droit de la preuve'. *C. de D.* 25 (1984): 50.
Nootens, S. 'La responsabilité civile du médecin anesthésiste'. RDUS 19 (1988): 55, 317.
Nootens, S. 'La relation médecin-patient et les décisions de traitement'. RDUS 20 (1990): 377.
Philips-Nootens, S., Kouri, R., & Lesage-Jarjoura, P. *Éléments de responsabilité médicale*, 4 edn. Cowansville: Éditions Yvon Blais, 2016.
Tôth, F. 'La responsabilité civile hospitalière pour la faute médicale: quand l'établissement hospitalier répond-il de la faute médicale'. In *Développements récents en droit de la santé*. Cowansville: Éditions Yvon Blais, 1991.

§5. Legal Practitioners

Archambault, J., *L'exercice anormal au droit d'ester en matière civile et sa sanction judiciaire*. Cowansville: Éditions Yvon Blais, 2005.
Bernard, P. 'La responsabilité des avocats en matière de procedure abusive'. RDUS 32 (2002): 272.
Borgia, D. 'La responsabilité civile de l'avocat'. In *Développements récents en droit immobilier*. Cowansville: Éditions Yvon Blais, 1996.
Jobin-Laberge, O. 'La responsabilité civile des avocats pour diffamation dans les actes de procédure'. In *Développements récents en droit civil*. Cowansville: Éditions Yvon Blais, 1993.
Jobin-Laberge, O. 'Le plaideur téméraire: gradation des sanctions'. In *Développements récents en déontologie et responsabilité professionnelle*. Cowansville: Éditions Yvon Blais, 1998.
Lacroix, M.E. *L'avocat diffamateur*. Cowansville: Éditions Yvon Blais, 2007.
Marquis, Y. *La responsabilité civile du notaire*. Cowansville: Éditions Yvon Blais, 1999.
Molinari, P. 'La responsabilité civile de l'avocat'. *R. du B.* 37 (1977): 275.

§6. Public Authorities

Archambault, J.D. *La responsabilité extracontractuelle de l'État: le politique et l'opérationnel*. Cowansville: Éditions Yvon Blais, 1996.
Bowal, P. & L. Boland. 'Crowning Glory: Liability in Negligence of Public Authorities Revisited'. RDUS 24 (1994): 435.
Garant, P. *L'action gouvernementale*. 3d edn. Cowansville: Éditions Yvon Blais, 2009.
Garant, P. *Droit administratif*. 6th edn. Cowansville: Éditions Yvon Blais, 2013.

Hogg, P. *Liability of the Crown*. 5th edn. Toronto: Carswell, 2012.
Ouellette, Y. 'Le recours en dommages contre le gouvernement et ses fonctionnaires'. RJT 26 (1992): 195.

§7. Abuse of Rights

Baudouin, J.-L. L'abus de droit d'ester en justice au Québec. In *Mélanges*. Camille Jauffret: Paris, Dalloz, 2013: 53.
Baudouin, J.-L. 'Abuse of Right in Quebec: Some 40 Years Later'. *La. L. Rev.* 76 (2016): 1185.
Jobin, P.-G. 'Grands pas et faux pas de l'abus de droit contractuel'. *C. de D.* 32 (1991): 153.
Lexop, R. 'L'abus de procédure en droit québécois'. Cowansville: Éditions Yvon Blais, 2015.
Morissette, Y. 'Abus de droit. Quérulence et parties non représentées'. *McGill L.J.* 49 (2004): 23.
Popovici, A. 'La poule et l'homme: sur l'Article 976 CcQ'. *R.du N.* 99 (1997): 214.

§8. Injury to Reputation and Privacy

Bouchard, J. 'L'indemnisation des victimes de harcèlement sexuel au Québec'. *C. de D.* 36 (1995): 125.
Brun, H. 'Liberté d'expression et de presse: droits à la dignité, l'honneur, la réputation et la vie privée'. RGD (1992): 449.
Cliche, B. and al. *Le harcèlement et les lésions psychologiques*, 2d edn., Cowansville: Éditions Yvon Blais, 2012.
Collection Yvon Blais. *La diffamation*. vol. 3, vol. 16, Cowansville: Éditions Yvon Blais, 2009, 2013.
Deleury, E. and D. Goubau. *Le droit des personnes physiques*. 5th edn. Cowansville: Éditions Yvon Blais, 2014.
Drapeau, M. *Le harcèlement sexuel: le régime de protection*. Cowansville: Éditions Yvon Blais, 1991.
Glenn, P. 'Le droit au respect de la vie privée'. *R. du B.* 39 (1979): 879.
Jukier, R. 'Non-pecuniary Damages in Defamation Cases'. *R. du B.* 49 (1989): 3.
Langevin, L. & N. Desrosiers. *L'indemnisation des victimes de violence sexuelle et conjugale*, 2nd edn. Cowansville: Éditions Yvon Blais, 2012.
Lebel, L. 'La protection des droits fondamentaux et la responsabilité civile'. *McGill L.J.* 231 (2004).
Molinari, P. & P. Trudel. 'Le droit au respect de l'honneur, de la réputation et de la vie privée: aspects généraux et applications'. Barreau du Québec, Application des chartes des droits et libertés en matière civile, Cowansville: Éditions Yvon Blais, 1988.
Morissette, R. *La presse et les tribunaux*. 2nd edn. Montréal: Wilson et Lafleur, 2004.

Potvin, L. *La personne et la protection de son image: étude comparative des droits québécois, français et de la common law anglaise*. Cowansville: Éditions Yvon Blais, 1991.
Sauriol, C. *Les abus de la liberté d'expression: l'encadrement juridique du rôle de critique*. Cowansville: Éditions Yvon Blais, 1993.
Vallières, N. *La presse et la diffamation*. Montréal: Wilson et Lafleur, 1985.

§9. LIABILITY OF PARENTS AND EDUCATORS

Boucher, J. 'Minorité et responsabilité, essai de sociologie juridique'. RJT 2 (1967): 437.
Desrosiers, N. 'La responsabilité de la mère pour le préjudice causé par son enfant'. *C. de D.* 36 (1995): 61.
Jobin, P.-G. 'La responsabilité présumée du père pour les dommages causés par son enfant mineur'. *R. du B.* 29 (1969): 570.
Mayrand, A. 'La présomption de faute du titulaire de l'autorité parentale et les diverses ordonnances de garde d'enfant'. *McGill L.J. 38* (1988): 257.

§10. LIABILITY OF EMPLOYERS

Goldstein, G. 'La responsabilité quasi-délictuelle du mandant pour la faute du mandataire en droit civil québécois'. RDUS 16 (1986): 123.
Masse, C. 'L'abus de fonctions dans la relation préposé-commettant en droit civil québécois'. *C. de D.* 19 (1978): 595.
Ménard, J. & D. Marin. *La responsabilité pour la faute d'autrui*. Cowansville: Éditions Yvon Blais, 1993.
Popovici, A. *La couleur du mandat*. Montréal, Thémis, 1995.

§11. LIABILITY OF THINGS UNDER ONE'S CARE

Antaki, K. 'Garde de structure et garde de comportement? - un aspect de la responsabilité du dommage causé par les choses'. *McGill L.J.* 12 (1966): 41.
Crépeau, P.-A. 'Liability for Damage Caused by Things from the Civil Law Point of View'. CBR 40 (1962): 222.
Millner, M. 'Autonomous Acts of Things in Quebec Law: Legal Adventurism Versus Legal Conservatism'. *McGill L.J.* 17 (1971): 699.

§12. LIABILITY FOR AUTOMOBILE ACCIDENTS

Baudouin, J.-L. 'La nouvelle législation québécoise sur les accidents de la circulation'. RIDC 31 (1979): 381.
Gardner, D. 'La loi sur l'assurance automobile, loi d'interprétation libérale?'. *C. de D.* 33 (1992): 485.

Gardner, D. 'L'interprétation de la portée de la Loi sur l'assurance automobile: un éternel recommencement'. In Moore B. (dir) *Mélanges Jean-Louis Baudouin*, Cowansville: Éditions Yvon Blais, 2012: 719.

Perreault, J. *L'indemnisation du préjudice corporel des victims d'accident d'automobile*. 2nd edn. Brossard: C.C.M.: 2005.

Perret, L. 'La nouvelle loi sur l'assurance automobile du Québec'. RGD 9 (1978): 7.

§13. Liability for Manufactured Products

Arbour, M.-E. 'Itinéraire du risque de développement à travers des codes et des constitutions'. In B. Moore (dir.), *Mélanges Jean-Louis Baudouin*. Cowansville: Éditions Yvon Blais, 2012: 677.

Crawford, W. 'Manufacturer's Liability under the Proposed Revision of the Civil Code of Quebec'. In *Conférence sur le nouveau Code civil du Québec*. Cowansville: Éditions Yvon Blais, 1999: 412.

Langlois, R. 'La responsabilité du fabricant en droit civil québécois: d'aujourd'hui à demain'. In *Conférence sur le nouveau Code civil*. Cowansville: Éditions Yvon Blais, 1991: 379.

Masse, C. 'La responsabilité du fabricant: responsabilité stricte, négligence, indemnisation sans égard à la faute?'. In *Conférence sur le nouveau Code civil du Québec*. Cowansville: Éditions Yvon Blais, 1992: 301.

Vézina, N. 'L'exonération fondée sur l'état des connaissances scientifiques et techniques dites du risque de développement.' In *Mélanges Claude Masse*, edited by C. Lafond. Cowansville: Éditions Yvon Blais, 2003.

§14. Limitation of Actions

Deslauriers, P. 'Recent Civil Law Developments in Extinctive Prescription'. In *Droit contemporain: rapports canadiens au Congrès international de droit compare*. Cowansville: Éditions Yvon Blais, 1995, 125.

Gervais, C. *La prescription*. Cowansville: Éditions Yvon Blais, 2009.

Jauffret-Spinosi, C. *Le temps et le droit*. Montréal: Thémis, 2007.

Langevin, L. & Desrosiers, N. 'L'impossibilité d'agir et les délais de prescription: lorsque le temps compte'. RJT 42 (2008): 395.

Lévesque, F. & C.-É. Wagner-Lapierre. 'La réforme de la prescription civile en matière d'infraction criminelle: une occasion manquée pour les victimes de préjudice corporel'. RJT 49 (2015).

Martineau, P. *La prescription*. Montréal: Presses de l'Université de Montréal, 1977.

McCann, J. 'Prescriptions extinctives et fins de non-recevoir'. Montréal: Wilson et Lafleur, 2011.

§15. CAUSATION

Brown, R. 'The Possibility of Inference Causation'. *McGill L.J.* 55 (2010) 1.
Gaudet, S. 'La perte de chance: un miroir aux alouettes?'. In *Mélanges Jean Pineau*. Montréal: Éditions Thémis, 2003.
Giroux, L. 'L'acceptation des risques'. *C. de D.* 9 (1968): 65.
Khoury, L. 'La responsabilité sans égard à la faute en matière médicale: impact sur le lien de causalité'. In accidents thérapeutiques et protection du consomateur, Cowansville: Éditions Yvon Blais, 2006: 283.
Khoury, L. *Uncertain Causation in Medical Liability*. Cowansville: Éditions Yvon Blais, 2006.
Khoury, L. 'Le juge canadien, anglais et australien devant l'incertitude causale en matière de responsabilité médicale'. McGill L.J. 59 (2014): 989.
Koury, R. 'La causalité et l'obligation de renseigner en droit médical québécois'. RDUS 17 (1987): 493.
Mayrand, A. 'L'énigme des fautes simultanées'. *R. du B.* 18 (1958): 1.
Nootens, S. 'La perte de chance: détournement du lien de causalité ou dommage distinct'. *R. du B.* 50 (1990): 611.

§16. EXCEPTION CLAUSES

Ferron, C. 'Les clauses de non-responsabilité en responsabilité civile contractuelle et délictuelle'. *R. du B.* 44 (1984): 3.
Moore, B. 'Les clauses abusives: dix ans après'. *R. du B.* 63 (2003): 59.
Sarna, B. *Traité de la clause de non-responsabilité*. Toronto: De Boo, 1975.

§17. DAMAGES

Baudouin, J.-L. 'Les dommages punitifs: un exemple d'emprunt réussi à la common law'. In *Mélanges Philippe Malinvaud*. Paris: Litec, 2007.
Bouchard, I. 'L'indemnisation des victimes de harcèlement sexuel au Québec'. *C. de D.* 36 (1995): 125.
Bruce, C.J. *Assessment of Personal Injury Damages*. 5th edn. Toronto: Butterworth, 11.
Cassels, J. & E. Adjin-Tettey. Remedies: The Law of Damage. Toronto: Irvin Law, 2008.
Charles, W. *A Handbook of the Assessment of Damages in Personal Injury Cases*. 2nd edn. Toronto: Carswell, 1990.
Cliche, B and al. Le harcèlement et les lésions psychologiques, 2nd edn. Cowansville: Éditions Yvon Blais, 2012.
Dallaire, C. *Les dommages exemplaires sous le régime des Chartes*. 2nd edn. Montréal: Wilson & Lafleur, 2003.

Deslauriers, P. 'La réparation du préjudice moral: pas et faux pas de la Cour suprême'. In *Développements récents en responsabilité civile.* Cowansville: Éditions Yvon Blais, 1997: 141.

Deslauriers, P. 'Les pertes non pécuniaires: compte rendu, constat, critique'. RJT 39 (2009): 371.

Drapeau, M. *Le harcèlement sexuel: le régime juridique de protection.* Cowansville: Éditions Yvon Blais, 1991.

Gardner, D. *L'évaluation du préjudice corporel.* 4th edn. Cowansville: Éditions Yvon Blais, 2016.

Gaudet, S. 'La perte de chance: un miroir aux alouettes?'. In *Mélanges Jean Pineau.* Montréal: Éditions Thémis, 2003.

Grammond, S. 'Un nouveau départ pour les dommages-intérêts punitifs'. R.G.D. 42 (2012): 105.

Karim, V. 'La réclamation des honoraires extrajudiciaires'. In Riendeau (éd.), 11 *Dire le droit: pour qui et à quel prix*, Montréal: Wilson et Lafleur, 2005.

Langevin, L., N. Deslauriers, & M. Nadeau. *L'indemnisation des victims de violences sexuelles et conjugale.* 2nd edn. Cowansville: Éditions Yvon Blais, 2012.

Morin, S. *Le dommage moral et le prejudice extrapatrimonial.* Cowansville: Éditions Yvon Blais, 2012.

Nootens, S. 'La perte de chance: détournement du lien de causalité ou dommage distinct?'. *R. du B.* 50 (1990): 611.

Popovici, A. 'Les dommages intérêts généraux'. In *Mélanges Jean-Louis Baudouin.* Cowansville: Éditions Yvon Blais, 2012: 891.

Pratte, P. 'Le rôle des dommages punitifs en droit québécois?'. *R. du B.* 59 (1999): 445.

Turgeon-Dorion, L. 'La qualification du préjudice civil en droit civil québécois'. R.J.T. 49 (2015): 133.

Selected Bibliography

Index

The numbers here refer to paragraph numbers.

Index

Index

www.ingramcontent.com/pod-product-compliance
Lightning Source LLC
Chambersburg PA
CBHW071354230926
51846CB00002B/551
9789403508412